THE TESTING AND LEARNING REVOLUTION

THE TESTING AND LEARNING REVOLUTION

THE FUTURE OF ASSESSMENT IN EDUCATION

Edmund W. Gordon and Kavitha Rajagopalan

First published 2016 by
PALGRAVE MACMILLAN

The authors have asserted their rights to be identified as the authors of this work in accordance with the Copyright, Designs and Patents Act 1988.

Palgrave Macmillan in the UK is an imprint of Macmillan Publishers Limited, registered in England, company number 785998, of Houndmills, Basingstoke, Hampshire, RG21 6XS.

Palgrave Macmillan in the US is a division of Nature America, Inc., One New York Plaza, Suite 4500, New York, NY 10004-1562.

Palgrave Macmillan is the global academic imprint of the above companies and has companies and representatives throughout the world.

Hardback ISBN: 978-1-137-51994-8
Paperback ISBN: 978-1-137-51995-5
E-PUB ISBN: 978-1-137-51997-9
E-PDF ISBN: 978-1-137-51996-2
DOI: 10.1057/9781137519962

Distribution in the UK, Europe and the rest of the world is by Palgrave Macmillan®, a division of Macmillan Publishers Limited, registered in England, company number 785998, of Houndmills, Basingstoke, Hampshire RG21 6XS.

Library of Congress Cataloging-in-Publication Data

Gordon, Edmund W., author.
    The testing and learning revolution : the future of assessment in education / Edmund W. Gordon and Kavitha Rajagopalan.
        pages cm
    Includes bibliographical references and index.
    ISBN 978-1-137-51994-8 (hardcover : alk. paper)
        1. Educational tests and measurements—United States.
    2. Teaching—United States. 3. Learning—United States. I. Rajagopalan, Kavitha, 1977–, author. II. Title.

LB3051.G595 2015
371.26—dc23   2015016086

A catalogue record for the book is available from the British Library.

To Kurt Landgraf, who supported the idea of the Gordon Commission on the Future of Assessment in Education, and to the thoughtful scholars who taught me and enabled me to lead it.

CONTENTS

Acknowledgments   ix

1 The Gordon Commission and a Vision for the Future
   of Assessment in Education   1

2 Assessment for Teaching and Learning, Not Just
   Accountability   9

3 Assessment Can and Should Incorporate Emerging
   Technologies and Epistemologies to Respond to
   Changing Paradigms in Education   35

4 Both Educating and Being Educated Are Changing
   in the Twenty-First Century   59

5 Assessment Requires Reasoning from Evidence   89

6 New Approaches to Assessment That Move in the
   Right Direction   107

7 New Data Collection and Analysis Methods Offer
   Powerful Insights into Performance   147

8 A Star to Guide By: Toward Assessment That Is
   Capable of Informing and Improving Teaching
   and Learning   169

Index   191

ACKNOWLEDGMENTS

In my conceptual memoir, *Pedagogical Imagination* (Third World Press, 2014), I candidly admit that in my unordinary long career, I have been intellectively parasitic. I have generated woefully few, if any, original ideas. I have freely borrowed, expanded upon, and/ or transformed the ideas of others. With respect to perspective, I have been particularly docile, as I have observed carefully, listened intently, and lived spongelike in intellectually rich and stimulating environments. Like Tennessee Williams's Blanche DuBois, "I have always depended on the kindness of [others]."

In none of my work has my docility been more obvious than in my leadership of the Gordon Commission on the Future of Assessment in Education. Under the leadership of Kurt Landgraf, the Education Testing Service (ETS) created and provided the financial support for the work of the commission. ETS then loaned to me consultative guidance from four of the holders of its five endowed chairs—Randy Bennett, Michael Kane, Robert Mislevy, and Michael Nettles. ETS supported the position of the executive officer of the commission, Paola C. Heincke, and a senior research associate, Rochelle Michel; in addition, I was allowed free access to counsel from Ida Lawrence, Joanna Gorin, Alina von Davier, Pascal Forgione, and L. Scott Nelson. I have no awareness of any other institution that has invited an independent group of scholars, funded them to critique, and made available as resources some of its most senior scholars. Even more foolhardy, Machiavellian, or plain courageous was the institution's decision to place the use of all of these resources at the discretion of a critical friend, known for his absence of expertise in measurement and very well known for his independence of thought. I am indebted to ETS for this opportunity, support, and trust. It is that generosity that has made the work of the Gordon Commission possible and has enabled the writing of *The Testing and Learning Revolution: The Future of Assessment in Education* (Palgrave Macmillan, 2015), which is my interpretation of that work.

I learned so much in the course of my leadership of the Gordon Commission. I will go to my grave still offering my thanks to the members of the Gordon Commission who served as much as my tutors as they served as my colleagues. The ideas captured here are my interpretation of what I learned from my interactions with my cochair Jim Pellegrino; executive councilmembers Eva Baker, Randy Bennett, Louis Gomez, Robert Mislevy, Lauren Resnick, and Lorrie Shepard; commissioners J. Lawrence Aber, Bruce Alberts, John Bailey, John Behrens, Ana Mari Cauce, Linda Darling-Hammond, Ezekiel Dixon-Román, James Paul Gee, Kenji Hakuta, Frederick Hess, Andrew Ho, Michael Martinez (dec.), Rodolfo Mendoza-Denton, Shael Polakow-Suransky, Diane Ravitch, Charlene Rivera, Lee Shulman, Elena Silva, Claude Steele, Ross Wiener, Robert Wise, and Constance Yowell; consultants to the chair Carl Kaestle, Lucius Outlaw, Sharon Lynn Kagan, and Kenneth Gergen; and consultants to the commission Jamal Abedi, Russell Almond, Eleanor Armour-Thomas, Lloyd Bond, A. Wade Boykin, John Bransford, Henry Braun, Tony Bryk, Li Cai, Robert Calfee (dec.), Madhabi Chatterji, Greg Chung, Dennis Culhane, Carol Dweck, Howard Everson, John Fantuzzo, Roy Freedle, Angela Glover-Blackwell, James Greeno, Kris Gutiérrez, Edward Haertel, David T. Hansen, Norris Haynes, Jeffery Henig, Cliff Hill, Stafford Hood, Gerunda Hughes, Daniel Koretz, Zeus Leonardo, Alan Lesgold, Charlie Lewis, Robert Lin, Robert McClintock, Raymond McDermott, Fayneese Miller, Luis C. Moll, Michelle Moody-Adams, Aaron Pallas, Thomas Payzant, David Pearson, Douglass Ready, Judith Singer, Mary Kay Stein, Donald Stewart, Hervé Varenne, Ernest Washington, Dylan Wiliam, John Willett, Mark Wilson, and Dennie Palmer Wolf.

"To Assess, to Teach, to Learn: A Vision for the Future of Assessment," the Gordon Commission's technical report, of which this book is a summative comment, is essentially a statement of some of what I learned from these thoughtful friends. I acknowledge with deep gratitude the assistance of Kavitha Rajagopalan, my editorial associate, in getting this message written in prose that can be widely understood. As she gained in her understanding of the measurement science and how it has been used in educational assessment, Kavitha was able to help me explain its limits and potential to a broader audience than currently concern themselves with these questions. Sarah Nathan, our editor at Palgrave Macmillan, has supported the publication of this work since her initial encounter with the material.

I wish that I could have written a scholarly treatise descriptive of what is to be done to better enable the sciences that inform assessment to best serve the needs and development of effective learning persons and those who teach them. Rather, what we have written is largely speculative and borders on wishful thinking. It has been observed that much of our thinking is more visionary—more a star to guide by than a blueprint. That may be because the field of measurement has dominated the field of assessment with a focus on the measurement of the status of learners' developed abilities. Our society has seen greater value in looking backward to see what we have done and who has achieved or not—in other words, knowing what students know—than it has been concerned with learning how to create ability—or, enabling learning and effective teaching. We believe that appropriate assessment *for* teaching and learning can inform and improve pedagogical processes and outcomes. Assessment can be analytic of process and can be educative.

We do not yet know how to do that well. But we acknowledge that we hear and see weak signals that the visions in the minds and works of a growing number of us are achievable. Guiding stars today, the blueprints are coming! We are grateful for the vision of what we believe is possible and the challenge to try.

EDMUND W. GORDON

1

THE GORDON COMMISSION AND
A VISION FOR THE FUTURE OF
ASSESSMENT IN EDUCATION

Conceptions of what it means to educate and to be an educated person are changing. The practice of the teaching and learning enterprise is broadening and expanding—as is what we demand of it. For many decades, we have focused our efforts at education reform and assessment on increasing accountability throughout the system of education—which has at the very least forced this dynamic and eclectic enterprise to constrict. Indeed, we may even have compromised the quality and capability of US education in the interest of meeting certain accountability criteria. At the same time, educational assessment has failed to incorporate or even respond to the many new developments in epistemology, the cognitive and learning sciences, as well as in pedagogical technologies. These realities are narrowing—possibly even stifling—creativity and flexibility in how we teach and learn. It was our growing concern about the long-term impact of this narrowing—and how it may limit us as a society from responding both to our democratic ideals as well as the very real challenges of the twenty-first-century marketplace—that led us to create the Gordon Commission on the Future of Assessment in Education at the generous invitation of then president and CEO of the Educational Testing Service, Kurt Landgraf. We convened in 2011, and as we began our inquiry, we also quickly came to the consensus that changing conceptions of—and practices in—educational assessment are making many of the capabilities of traditional conceptions and practices in educational assessment obsolete. The work of the commission rests on the assumption that assessment in education can, and indeed should, inform and improve teaching and learning processes and outcomes.

Over the two years it was active, the commission sought to distill and connect the transformative ideas of leading and creative minds from a number of disciplines and emerged with a set of core issues and ideas. Those notions were never interwoven into a single text that might be communicated to a broader audience of stakeholders in the education enterprise—not just scholars of pedagogy and measurement science. This book is the attempt to interpret the concerns of the Gordon Commission to the very diverse community of stakeholders in the education enterprise and educational testing.

The education of our children concerns every person in the United States—they are our greatest resource and our strongest buttress against the torrential changes heading our way in the twenty-first century, such as changes in how the United States interacts in the global community, changes in how we live and work, changes in how we respond to growing mobility and diversity, and changes in the availability of data and how it affects our lives. And yet, the prevailing tone in the debate around education reform is rife with blame and accusation—the stuff of short-term politics. With this book and the work of the commission that informed it, we wish to move the debate around education reform away from this unproductive line and toward a conversation in which we apply the wealth of scholarship on how people think and learn toward enabling all learners in the United States. to become the most intellectively developed they can be. We believe that, with a simple shift in perception, we can begin to reenvision assessment not just as a tool for measuring students and sorting them along a hierarchy for the purposes of holding students, teachers, and even entire school systems accountable, but instead as a tool to help us understand the processes of teaching and learning and to improve the quality of our educational interventions—so that we may enable all students to develop to the full extent of their native-born ability. We believe that all students—regardless of race, linguistic background, socio-economic status, family life, whether they live in a city or country or suburb, whether they are well-fed or hungry, or any other way we choose to divide our learner population—are capable of learning and achieving what I call full "intellective competence" (a concept I discuss in detail in chapter 4, which generally refers to a capacity and disposition to adapt to, appreciate, know, and understand the phenomena of human experience to make sense of the world). The challenge for our education system is not to determine whether or even why a student has failed to achieve but rather to enable that student to learn and develop as fully as she is able, so that she may navigate the world around her, live a full life, and yes, contribute as fully as she is able to her society. So, although this book and its contents are the business of every single person who is invested in the education of our children, in the interest of effecting the most rapid and wide-ranging transformation, we are speaking here to you, the people who are capable of influencing and transforming how we view, use, construct, and practice assessment in education today.

The primary objective of the book is to convey how we may employ existing and emerging technologies, ideas, and theories toward responding to the pedagogical and assessment challenges of the twenty-first century, and how we may incorporate long-accepted ideas from the behavioral sciences into the practice of educational assessment. While many of these ideas—such as the importance of context and perspective—are beginning to be accepted and practiced in the behavioral sciences, they are relatively new to the field of measurement sciences, which historically has actively sought to remove both the test taker and the task being tested from any real-life context. This is one of the most radical and significant contributions of this work: it challenges education policy makers and practitioners to allow assessment to benefit from a broader range of well-developed epistemological scholarship, as well as from relevant emerging technologies, in order to address long-standing flaws in our educational assessment and to more effectively meet the needs of learning and teaching in the twenty-first century. The Gordon Commission on the Future of Assessment in Education has attempted to synthesize emerging scholarship in the many disciplines and practices that have meaningful guidance for the field of assessment and to initiate a society-wide dialogue on how we may begin to shift from assessment *of* education (where we have been and what we have achieved) to assessment *for* education (how teaching and learning function and can be improved).

The conversation has begun. In the two years since the commission concluded, its message has been disseminated far and wide in scholarly circles. Its papers have been abstracted, excerpted, republished, and expanded upon in some of the country's leading journals in education and pedagogy, and there is some initial discussion underway of creating a permanent, standing committee on the future of assessment for education at the National Academy of Education. At the same time, the ideas encapsulated in the Gordon Commission's body of work, which are generated, supported, and endorsed by leading thinkers in the field of education, will require a great effort to adopt into practice. With the adoption and rollout of the Common Core State Standards in the humanities and the forthcoming standards in science, we have both the public's attention and sense of urgency focused on educational assessment. While we on the commission applaud the Common Core's focus on the development of so-called higher-order thinking and twenty-first-century competencies, we maintain that efforts to assess whether these competencies *have* been developed will still fall far short of assessment's potential to help enable the development of these competencies. Recent high-profile cheating scandals and resistance to standardized testing of these new standards serve as poignant evidence that there is society-wide resistance to assessing as we have been doing, even if we change the targets of these assessments. This resistance invites us to approach assessment with new eyes, so that we see assessment not just as it is but as it could be. It is to this end that we offer this book—a conversation piece, an inspiration, a motivation, a north star by which we, the stakeholders in the education enterprise and influencers of education policy can, in the words of M. K. Gandhi, be the change we wish to see in the world.

AN INTRODUCTION TO THE GORDON COMMISSION

The Gordon Commission was created with the mission to study the best of educational assessment policy, practice, and technology; consider the best estimates of what education will become and what will be needed from educational measurement during the twenty-first century; and to generate recommendations on educational assessment design and application that meet and/or exceed the demands and needs of education—present and predicted. In brief, the goals of the Gordon Commission were as follows:

- Inform the field and the public about the need and possibilities for change in education, as well as change in the functions, practices, and roles of assessment in education
- Increase public awareness and knowledge about assessment as an integral component of education and the possibilities for change in assessment practice
- Encourage the field of educational assessment to strengthen its capacity to factor into measurement practice attention to the influence of human attributes, social contexts, and personal identities on human performance
- Balance emphasis on prediction, selection, and accountability with equal concern for informing and improving teaching and learning processes and outcomes
- Inform long-term planning and product development in the field of psychometrics

The Gordon Commission consisted of 30 members: 2 chairpersons, 6 executive council members, and 22 commissioners. Over the course of our 2 years of active inquiry, we engaged 4 consultants from the fields of history, philosophy, policy, and psychology to advise the chairpersons, 51 consultants to the entire commission, and 10 staffers to help us organize, manage, and produce the many projects, publications, and activities of the commission. The scholars, policy makers, and practitioners who comprised the commission identified critical issues concerning educational assessment, investigated those issues, and developed position and review papers that informed the commission's recommendations for policy and practice in educational assessment. An overview of the how the commission brought these various persons together to over its two-year period, as well as the many projects, papers, and initiatives it generated, can be found in the commission's technical report (see Gordon et al., 2013).

FROM MY PERSPECTIVE ON ASSESSMENT AND TOWARD A NEW VISION FOR ASSESSMENT IN EDUCATION

My own perspective on assessment in education became the starting point for the commission's inquiries and critiques and is summarized in brief below:

- Traditional approaches to testing overemphasize the status of a narrow range of cognitive functions in learners and neglect to consider what psychologists refer to as the affective and situative domains of human performance and the processes by which these functions and domains are engaged.

- Current assessment instruments and procedures tend to neglect the diverse contexts and perspective born of different cultural experiences and cultural identities and the influence of these contexts, perspectives, and identities on human performance. While some important features of intellective competence may require than the expression of competence be demonstrated independent of such contexts, perspectives, and identities, other components and features are very much associated with these conditional correlates.

- Traditionally, testing has privileged—in its purposes—accountability, prediction, and selection to the neglect of diagnosis, prescription, and the informing and improving of teaching and learning processes and outcomes. I believe that the most important functions and purposes of measurement in education concern informing, as well as improving, teaching and learning processes and outcomes.

- Traditional approaches to assessment have emphasized relative position and competition to the neglect of criterion-based judgments of competence. The meritocratic ideology that dominates in testing may be dysfunctional to developmental democratization, particularly when developmental opportunities are distributed on the basis of prior developmental achievements and when level of prior development may be, in part, a function of the maldistribution of the opportunity to develop, learn, or excel.

- Traditional approaches to assessment privilege knowing, knowing how to, and mastery of knowledge that is held to objectively "true" or "real," while intellective competence, emerging epistemologies, and the cohabitation of populations with diverse cultural forms may—increasingly—require multiple ways of knowing, understanding as well as knowing, and the ability to adjudicate competing relationships in our knowledge and in the production of knowledge.

• The pursuit of content mastery should be in the service of the development of mental processes. Michael Martinez's (2000) notions in his book, *Education as the Cultivation of Intelligence*, resonate with me. Michael's mentor, the late Richard Snow, left an incomplete idea in which he was developing the argument for the study of content (subject matter) as instrumental to the development of intellect (Snow, 1986). I am attracted to the notion of the study of any content as a means of nurturing intellect, as well as for the purposes of knowing.

In this book, I explore the central ideas of the Gordon Commission in a progression, beginning with a chapter that lays out the concept of assessment *for* education. This is followed by a chapter that discusses the period of tremendous transformation and flux into which we are entering—changing paradigms in education, emerging epistemologies and technologies, and expanding sociopolitical imperatives for equity in excellence in a diverse learner population—and how assessment and measurement sciences have to date failed to respond to or incorporate these changes. Chapter 4 explores what it will mean to be an educated person in this century, introducing readers to two possible conceptualizations of what an educated person should have achieved through his education—Bereiter and Scardamalia's (2012) conception of "knowledgeability" and my own conception of "intellective competence." Chapter 5 introduces a powerful conceptualization of assessment as an evidence gathering and analysis enterprise, interrogating how we have viewed and can shift our view of sources and forms of evidence in assessment, and how these various forms of evidence must be orchestrated in the effort to make a judgment or decision about education. The next chapter then introduces the reader to new ways in which current assessment data (from summative, standardized tests) may be analyzed in the service of improving teaching and learning, as well as new forms of assessment that move us further along the spectrum toward what Eleanor Armour-Thomas and I (2012) call "dynamic pedagogy," which weaves assessment, teaching, and learning into a single cloth and seeks to enable intellective competence (and not just the ability to succeed at tests) in all learners. Chapter 7 introduces us to the concept of relational data analysis, and how data (or, evidence from assessment) may be viewed in relation to each other in decision making about education. We conclude with a chapter that lays out a guide by which future efforts at shifting from assessment *of* toward assessment *for* education may be undertaken.

Just as education is not merely the business of educators and learners, so too we suggest that assessment is not merely the business of test designers and administrators on the one hand or the test takers on the other, but can be a powerful and dynamic tool for effecting real transformation in how we view and deliver education in our society today and in the future.

BIBLIOGRAPHY

Armour-Thomas, E., & Gordon, Edmund W. (2012). *Toward an understanding of assessment as a dynamic component of pedagogy.* Princeton, NJ: Educational Testing Service. http://www.gordoncommission. org/rsc/pdf/armour_thomas_gordon_understanding_assessment.pdf

Bereiter, C., & Scardamalia, M. (2012). *What will it mean to be an educated person in the mid-21st century?* Princeton, NJ: Educational Testing Service. http://www.gordoncommission.org/rsc/pdfs/bereiter_scardamalia_what_will_mean_educated_person_century.pdf

Gordon, Edmund W., et al. (2013). *To assess, to teach, to learn: A vision for the future of assessment: Technical report.* Princeton, NJ: Educational Testing Service. http://gordoncommission.org/rsc/pdfs/gordon_commission_technical_report.pdf

Gordon, E. Wyatt, Gordon, Edmund W., Aber, J. L., & Berliner, D. (2012). *Changing paradigms for education: From filling buckets to lighting fires to cultivation of intellective competence.* Princeton, NJ: Educational Testing Service. http://www.gordoncommission.org/rsc/pdf/gordon_gordon_berliner_aber_changing_paradigms_education.pdf

Martinez, M. (2000). *Education as the cultivation of intelligence.* New York: Routledge.

Snow, R. E. (1977). Individual differences and instructional theory. *Educational Researcher, 6,* 11–15.

2

ASSESSMENT FOR TEACHING
AND LEARNING, NOT JUST
ACCOUNTABILITY

In the United States today, nearly 50 years after the publication of perhaps the most influential education study, the Coleman et al. report (1966), "Equality of Educational Opportunity," which among other things attempted to investigate the achievement gap between black and white students in segregated America, we still struggle to achieve universal high-quality educational outcomes in diverse populations. We are only just beginning to understand diversity as a far more complex and universal phenomenon than black and white; today, American students come not only from many racial, ethnic, religious, and linguistic backgrounds but, like people in all societies, they also come from different socioeconomic backgrounds and family configurations, learn in different ways, and see the world through their own unique lenses. In a society as large and complex as ours, we struggle to attain our relatively recent democratic goal of delivering high-quality educational opportunities to all students. The ongoing effort to achieve this goal has not only led to the proliferation of alternatives to public education but has also undergirded the creation of universal standards and curricula as well as a national system of educational assessment.

In America today, we test simply to assess the productivity of the educational system. This is not helping us to improve the quality of education for our diverse student populations. If our primary question of educational assessment is whether we are doing well, this kind of measurement exercise is moot. We already know the answer to this question: we are failing. Instead, in the act of assessment, we must ask more visceral and illuminating questions. Indeed, we can and should use the measurement sciences to understand the very processes by which abilities are developed, and, in turn, how all students in our diverse learner population can be as well educated as they are able to be, and prepared for the challenges of the twenty-first century. We should be investing in a system of assessment that serves the purposes of education, not one that measures the effects of education. In other words, we can and should be conducting assessment *for* rather than *of* education.

For most of the twenty-first century, we have been aware of the underproductivity of our schooling. At best, we have brought some 60 percent of our students to a level of expected competence as measured by current tests, and have failed to reduce dropout rates, particularly among low-income and minority students. As the standards for what I call intellective competence (a concept I introduced in chapter 1 and discuss at length in chapter 4) have risen and become more complex under the new Common Core State Standards, and presumably by the new array of assessments developed to measure them, the goal of achieving universal competence of US students seems more and more out of reach. We have explained away our inadequate system of education by pointing to increasing diversity among school-aged children, a phenomenon that is not at all a unique to the United States. In fact, diversity of learner population is a challenge for most countries worldwide. Whether a society makes distinctions between segments of its population by race, class, language, or any other—often arbitrary— system of categorization, we find that the greater the difference between groups, the worse the achievement outcomes. From this, we can conclude that our problem is creating effective systems of public education that serve people who differ in all kinds of ways.

The measurement sciences can serve as just the investigative tool we need to understand and eventually solve this problem. Instead, we have responded to this general problem by demanding more of schooling, by increasing its mechanisms of accountability, and by depending more and more on the data from standardized tests of academic achievement. A competitive and punitive approach to accountability has emerged as a principal component of national state-level education policies, based largely on the data from these standardized tests. Even where states have envisioned supports for teachers and students, the fluctuation of their financial and political bases have made these plans maddeningly unstable.

Reflecting on the work of my colleagues on the Gordon Commission, I assert that measurement science can do far more to help us improve educational outcomes if we align it with more enlightened educational policies. Certainly, accountability is a very important objective but there are many more things we desire and demand of our education system and new scholarship is showing us that the uses of assessment can be expanded to help us meet these objectives as well. We can improve how we measure academic achievement with assessments that are more inclusive and have demonstrably greater validity for the range of students, settings, and purposes to be served. If our goal is indeed to improve educational outcomes, we strengthen our chances of success by incorporating new and emerging learning concepts, research findings, and technologies. It is now possible to use measurement science to analyze, document, and appraise the teaching and learning processes, so their results can inform teaching and learning. There is one caveat: the assessments themselves must have value. Indeed, in most instances, measurement and assessment can and should be part of instruction. Measurement science should be as concerned with the cultivation of intellective and affective abilities as it has traditionally been with the measurement of developed ability.

There are two major points we wish to make in this chapter. Instead of assessment *of* education as a single goal of testing, we should be striving for assessment *for* education—or, assessment in the service of teaching and learning. In this, I am advocating for a system of education that weaves measurement, tests, and assessment into the educational fabric and adjusts and evolves to account for learning, context, attribution, new knowledge and values, and public policy. To do this, measurement must be fashioned anew.

HISTORY OF ASSESSMENT IN EDUCATION

In an illuminating history of assessment in the United States prepared for the Gordon Commission, former president of the

National Academy of Education and renowned education historian Carl Kaestle (2012) wrote that testing in the United States has not always been standardized exercises used for high-stakes decisions. These came about in the mid-nineteenth century, when Horace Mann led a reformist movement to centralize education, pushing for periodic written tests. There was widespread opposition to standardized testing even then, with critics decrying the focus on memorization over understanding, but even when critics succeeded in having a test phased out, it was often merely replaced by another test.

Parallel to this development, he writes, early professional psychologists sought to explain correlations as a way to provide comparable measures of accomplishment in a radically centralized educational system. Inspired by discoveries in genetics, many researchers set about to find a person's summary and presumably inherited level of intelligence. Working along a different line of inquiry, Alfred Binet developed scales of increasing item difficulty in order to assist in the classification of children along a timeline of "normal" development. Synthesizing the hereditarian tradition and Binet's scales, Lewis Terman adapted and popularized the term "intelligence quotient" (IQ), a figure derived by dividing the mental age score by the subject's chronological age. Terman's production of the Stanford-Binet intelligence test brought him fame as the president of the American Psychological Association. He used IQ tests to promote eugenicist ideas, including immigration restrictions and sterilization of low-IQ people. Later, during World War I, IQ tests were used to classify army recruits until the military discontinued their use over objections about their utility for measuring the intelligence of non-English speakers.

Despite these troubling origins, writes Kaestle, public schools embraced IQ testing, which appealed to educators' regard for efficient and scientific decision making about teachers and students in an era of larger systems and greater student diversity. In 1920, its first year, the National Intelligence Test sold 200,000 copies. Contemporary critics questioned the heritability and immutability of IQ, which was used to justify racist and sexist positions proclaiming the mental inferiority of blacks to whites or women to men.

In the early twentieth century, continues Kaestle, achievement testing emerged, morphing into a standardized testing movement. Unlike IQ tests, achievement tests had diverse subject matter, provided comparative data across classrooms and schools, and made narrower claims about ability and its origins, and were therefore less vulnerable to criticism. An industry grew up around these tests, which were scored by hand in the early years but eventually by machine. Testing research and development drove the discourse of professional educators. Colleges were drawn into the testing regime and the College Board was established to develop standards and standardized examinations for college entrance. The Scholastic Aptitude Test (SAT) was a direct descendant of the Army Alpha intelligence test from World War I and was immediately put to work—against the College Board's advice—in predicting later college performance. The test's developer, Carl Brigham (1923), tried to distance the test from IQ testing and opposed its implementation as a major college admissions test. Standing at the mid-ground between intelligence and achievement tests, the SAT became and has remained very influential in college admissions.

Following World War II, Kaestle writes, the United States emerged as a new superpower with a growing education system and research sector. Efforts to institute a meritocracy within schools relied on an expansion of testing to provide evidence for sorting decisions. Despite some critiques that testing was biased against the working class, the use of tests continued to expand in the late 1950s. The activist 1960s phase of the civil rights movement brought a concern for equity to the targeted testing to ensure that schools were serving different groups well. Worries about the disparate impact of tests on diverse groups of students led to a decrease in the use of some tests for placement, along with legal and advocacy efforts to eliminate cultural bias in other tests like the SAT. The focus shifted from equal opportunities to equal outcomes. Reducing the achievement gap became a primary goal, in some cases a substitute for school integration. This would require holding teachers, schools, and districts accountable for their results, which prompted the drafting of the National Assessment of Educational Progress in the Kennedy administration.

This was just one of several efforts during the 1960s identified by Kaestle that advanced the idea of basing policy decisions on student-learning measures: in 1965, Robert Kennedy introduced an amendment to the Elementary Secondary Education Act requiring districts serving poor and minority students to devise their own tests and the same year, President Johnson implemented the Pentagon's Planning-Programming-Budgeting System (PPBS) system requiring independent performance analyses for all government agencies.

Kaestle points out that the emphasis on outcomes was further reinforced by the Coleman report. The report's massive statistical study—a landmark both in methodology and in policy implications—concluded that schools' physical resources were less important to a student's achievement than their family background and class, the ability of their teachers, and students' belief in their ability to control their fate. The report questioned the utility of spending resources on schools and implied that social-class integration was more important than race per se. The report had little political impact, due to obfuscation by the Office of Education and resistance by educators, but it had long-term influence on the educational research community because of its quantitative focus and implication that schools cannot solve social problems alone. Throughout the 1970s, civil rights movements continued to win new victories in establishing bilingual education, banning sex discrimination in education programs receiving federal funds, and encouraging participation of children with disabilities in regular classrooms, all of which increased the amount and significance of testing.

Amid growing anxiety about competitiveness, fueled in part by the National Commission on Excellence in Education (1983) report, "A Nation at Risk," and increased gubernatorial interest in their own states' performance, state-level achievement testing had become one of the main instruments of reform in the 1980s, writes Kaestle. Proponents argued that high-quality tests would be worth "teaching to" while critics insisted that pervasive high-stakes testing inevitably led to test-savvy drilling in disconnected bits of knowledge. The debate turned on an anomaly in American testing: the ubiquitous multiple-choice question reflects a behaviorist theory of learning that hasn't been in the psychological mainstream since the 1950s. The ascent of cognitive psychology transformed the field and influenced curriculum development but was not reflected in assessment practice.

The 1990s saw the development of two important frameworks for assessment policy: standards-based reform (SBR), which has become the mainstream policy, and performance assessment, which faced considerable challenges, continues Kaestle. SBR is based on content standards that define what students should know and performance standards that define by when students should be able to perform what tasks with that knowledge, and promises alignment with instruction and assessment and to serve the goals of both excellence and equity. Performance assessments promise to combat the practice of teaching to the low-level skills emphasized by multiple-choice tests but are more costly and threaten existing standardization frameworks, raising questions about comparability. Both presidents Clinton and George W. Bush championed standards-based reform. The civil rights aspect of assessment focused on provisioning more resources to underperforming schools and demographic groups under Bush's No Child Left Behind (NCLB) earned the act bipartisan support. Although President Obama declared many aspects of NCLB unproductive, both his and the Bush administrations have promoted a framework of standards-based reform with strong federal oversight. SBR is bolstered by considerable bipartisan consensus but criticism of the narrowing of curricula under excessive testing is widespread among both academics and teachers.

Bringing his historic account to the present day, Kaestle writes that, among other reforms, the Obama administration has required that states join multistate consortia to develop new standards and assessments, the largest group of which has proposed the set of aligned standards and assessments that make up the Common Core State Standards. The Common Core State Standards evades fears about federal control due to its *national but not federal* nature. Many administrators and other stakeholders are drawn to the economy of scale promised by many states working together to develop complicated standards and assessments. The leaders of Common Core State Standards aspire to first-rate standards and assessments but some of the most complicated aspects of the envisioned assessments require more test time or the use of computers. Many states and districts are resisting these features. Common Core State Standards and their assessments are a work in progress. Judgments on their effectiveness will not be possible for several years and it remains to be seen if the political will and organizational capacity exist for school systems to reduce achievement gaps without broader social and economic reforms.

In the conclusion to his extensive account, Kaestle observes that assessment policy is necessarily a struggle between competing values. Standardized multiple-choice tests of basic skills have limitations for teaching higher-order thinking and representing diverse student capabilities but they serve important equity and accountability goals by describing patterns of comparable performance across individuals and groups. Nonetheless, a new balance is needed between these different goals. Present testing practices have powerful support because many people accept them as defining educational accomplishment. They are cheap and appeal to the popular priority placed on factual knowledge as a primary purpose of schooling. Over time, those testing practices have been expanded to make judgments about different stakeholders, from individual students to teachers, schools, districts, states, and entire demographic groups. Test practices have changed over time—to a limited extent—to reflect evolving concepts of what intelligence is and what skills we wish to foster in our students. But an abiding continuity is the use of standardized, multiple-choice or short-answer test items. Still, if we wish to evolve testing to advance our democratic value of high-quality education for all learners in our society, we must begin to see assessment as far more—and far more integral a piece of pedagogy—than simple, affordable standardized tests that generate data used primarily for the purpose of accountability.

In a powerful paper for the Gordon Commission, Herve Varenne (2012) describes how public education (and its assessment) has not only failed to respond to the philosophical ideals of Horace Mann and John Dewey (1897/1959) that led to its establishment as a modern democratic institution but has, in fact, also created another mechanism for systemic discrimination. He writes that curriculum, pedagogy, and education in the humanistic sense, are all to the good but the core political issue is that assessments have often led to improperly produced and publicly proclaimed privilege. Further in the paper, he observes that, at the beginning of the second decade in the twenty-first century, philosophers, researchers, policy makers, and activists know that things are not working out quite as Mann, and many others around the world, dreamed the common, public, free, compulsory school would work. Even as this vision of school has spread around the globe, critics worldwide point out how achievement gaps remain and how birth privilege has been reproducing itself. Most of us hope, he writes, that all that is needed is a further refinement of these processes. And so we must assess the assessments and imagine new ones. He calls for imagining assessments that leverage what actually happens while preserving the "government's duty" to see to it that the "means of education are provided for all" (paraphrase of Mann, 1846/1957, p. 63). This possible institution might still look like schooling but it would not be in the business of granting rights and privileges.

Through Varenne's critique, we can see that the current system of education and assessment in the United States has not only failed to achieve the democratic ideal of public education but is, in fact, also reproducing discrimination. If the imperative of education in the twenty-first century is to make available and deliver high-quality education to all learners in the population, Varenne's position is both a searing and terribly urgent call to action. At the Gordon Commission, we reached the conclusion that an effective action toward righting this wrong would be to change the way we assess, so that our assessment does not validate and make permanent inequality but rather enables educators and educational institutions to respond to the individual needs of learners and enable the success of all. To this end, we have developed a plan for transforming assessment of education into assessment *for* education.

FROM A HISTORY OF ASSESSMENT *OF* EDUCATION TO ASSESSMENT *FOR* EDUCATION

The history of assessment in education in human societies has largely been an effort to document the status, describe the characteristics, and measure the achievements of learning persons. The status of a learner's characteristics or abilities has primarily been used to measure the effect of—or the need for—education. This long history has resulted in the emergence of a highly developed system of science of the measurement of education. This science and its techniques have been embraced in the business of predicting, selecting, and allocating certification. But assessment of education has not been as effective as instrumentation for informing and improving teaching and learning. Because assessment has emphasized measurement of status, it has concurrently neglected attention to teaching and learning processes, the potential capacities of the learner, and the process of becoming that which is at the heart of the teaching and learning transaction. Assessment, we well know, has a tremendous potential to offer invaluable insight into all of these processes.

The Gordon Commission's concern with assessment *for* education is by no means new. Shortly after Binet produced his model for intelligence testing in an effort to assist in sorting out educable from uneducable students, he wrote a greatly neglected essay (1916) concerning the responsibility of a society capable of identifying those considered to be uneducable, for doing something to help those described as so limited. Western European nations and the United States, preoccupied with World War I and the selection of talent for that effort, embraced Binet's instrument for the assessment of and ignored his recommendation of the need for assessment for education.

Some 50 years later, Else Haeussermann, Herbert Birch, and I, challenged by the desire and need to plan education for children who had suffered damage to the central nervous examination, developed an elaborate procedure for the assessment (evaluation) of educational potential in brain-damaged children (Haeussermann, 1958). We set out to design a set of procedures that could describe and document the processes by which children engaged with academic learning; not so much what they could not do or what they knew how to do but how they went about using or not using what they had. We were intent upon providing teachers with information that would be used by teachers to inform and improve the teaching and learning transactions for which they were responsible. Rather than measurement against standardized benchmarks, we sought to determine the conditions under which certain benchmarks could be reached. In what contexts could certain problems be recognized and engaged? Teachers found the clinical reports from these assessments for informing and improving education to be enormously helpful but we who developed these report found the production to be excessively labor intensive. Our fellow psychologists objected to the absence of any metrics by which individual children could be compared to other children.

Working and writing at about the same time as Haeussermann was Mary Meeker who, in her despair at all of the information available from standardized tests that was left unused, developed a set of templates that could be used to analyze the data from standardized tests so as to reveal the indications of mental activity that lay camouflaged in the data of some standardized achievement tests (Meeker, 1965). When Barbara Messick and I revisited this work, we tried to unbundle selected test items to reveal the nature of the intellective demands behind the items (Gordon, 1970). We theorized that this information, made available to teachers, could be used to help students better understand the meaning of the test item as well as the appropriateness and inappropriateness of the student's approach to the problem. Unfortunately, changes in circumstances and interest precluded continued work on this set of problems but interest in the paradigm has persisted.

While the primary body of work produced by the Gordon Commission focuses on the assessment of education, we were also tasked with forecasting a future for assessment in education. As we looked into the crystal ball, and even as we observed forerunners of the future, it became clear that while much has been and can be learned from the continued assessment of education, rapidly emerging developments in education and its assessment will both demand and enable assessment that is in the service of informing and improving teaching and learning processes and outcomes.

TOWARD A NEW APPROACH TO ACCOUNTABILITY

We are currently in a pivotal period in the field of education and education reform in the United States. Fortunately, despite one of the most serious economic downturns in recent history, we see widespread recognition of the critical importance assigned to more effective approaches to education. Given the considerable body of research findings that document the correlation between socioeconomic status and academic achievement, it is troubling that except for the brief and insufficient effort at the "war on poverty," little or no attention is given to improvement in family conditions of life as an approach to improving educational outcomes. As discussed, the Coleman report concluded in 1966 that the greatest amount of variance in academic achievement was associated with the stability and quality of the home life of students. And yet, this decades-old and growing body of research has largely been ignored in the national debate on education reform, which appears to focus on how to hold schools, teachers, and to some extent, students accountable for the quality of academic achievement. Logical though this may seem, the facts appear to point to an alternative conclusion.

Given the absence of any substantial evidence to support the use of data from standardized tests to hold any specific group accountable for levels of academic achievement, we need alternative approaches to accountability. Borrowing from a public health model, a viable alternative may be to stress responsibility over punitive approaches to accountability. Some of us are giving thought to more productive usages that could be made of educational assessment data. We argue that assessment processes and their data could be better used to inform and improve teaching and learning processes and outcomes.

This punitive use of the data from standardized tests for purposes of holding students and their administrators and teachers accountable may be eroding confidence in the education enterprise. As instances of cheating are uncovered with increasing frequency, not only by students but also by administrators and teachers for self-advancement and for self-protection, it will be difficult for any of us to maintain confidence in that system of education. As the pressure of punitive accountability increases and effort is more and more directed at gaming the system rather than at improved teaching and learning, the outcomes of these endeavors are more likely to suffer than to improve.

Almost 50 years ago, the distinguished education historian Lawrence Cremin (1975/2007) advocated for thinking comprehensively about education. We interpret such a comprehensive approach to mean that education includes all of the education relevant experiences and resources to which one is exposed in life— good health and nutrition, stimulating environments, talking and reading with children beginning at an early age, preschool education, family trips, museums, libraries, faith-based institutions, guidance and tutorial services, space and time to study, family and community expectations, and support for academic and personal development. A national policy of education cannot be limited to rigid demands for accountability and exclusive attention to school reform. A rational national policy concerning education must be comprehensive in its scope.

As I have begun to reeducate myself on developments in the field of educational assessment, I have realized that the field consists of conceptual and methodological issues. I think the field has tried to attend to both, but it has privileged outdated theories of human behavior that were extant at the time the field first began to emerge. The growing use of measurement for the purposes of accountability in education throughout the twentieth century forced the entrenchment and institutionalization of methods that were informed by those theories—validity, reliability, standardization, and quantification of abilities.

When we turn to the future of this field, we must bear in mind that there are emerging conceptualizations about human behavior and newer theories about how to enable human development— and to ensure that such development is taking place during the teaching and learning processes. We must also consider what kinds of theories may emerge 50 years from now. They are certainly not likely to be the notions we held in 1875 or 1920. Perhaps the notions prevalent in 2000 will have accumulated cobwebs by 2050. Just as relativity challenges veridicality (or the assertion of a single truth), so too do string theory and randomization challenge the concept of predictability. Chaos theory is increasingly used to describe the natural state, where we once sought to uncover the orderly relationships between things in nature. Our heavy dependence on mechanical metaphors is being forced to consider the utility of organic metaphors. The methodological concerns of our founders may not be useful to us as we seek to think about what assessment will be like in another 50 years.

Given that we cannot rationally hold schools, teachers, and students alone accountable for academic achievement, given that the theoretical underpinnings of how we currently practice assessment are wildly outmoded, and given that there is little evidence that high-stakes testing has improved teaching and learning outcomes, we may conclude that it is a mistake in national and state education policy to continue the heavy dependence on the use of current approaches to standardized testing for high-stakes purposes to drive a punitive system of accountability for teaching and learning. I can think of no substantial body of research that supports the idea that we can force teachers to succeed at teaching or students to succeed at learning by negative reenforcement (punishment). Similarly, I have not seen the evidence that even suggests that the standardized testing of the status of students' abilities contributes to our understanding of more than the status of the possible outcomes of teaching and learning. Such data do little to inform what should be done to teach better or to learn better. Penalizing teachers or students for failure to succeed at either is certainly dysfunctional and may even be immoral, given the weak association between such testing, teaching, and learning.

THE NEW COMMON CORE STATE STANDARDS: MOVING FROM PUSHBACK TO EMBRACING OPPORTUNITY

The introduction of the new Common Core State Standards has reignited a very important national debate on education. There is widespread restiveness over the inappropriate use of standardized tests to drive high-stakes decisions on pedagogical policies and practices. Understandably, there is also a great deal of concern and confusion about the new standards for the outcomes of education and skepticism about new tests based on these standards, which seem more difficult than previous tests. Given recent revelations about privacy, many people are concerned about how data from these tests might be used, especially to make highly consequential decisions concerning individual students, teachers, and schools, as well their seemingly indelible residence in cyberspace. Finally, many sense that too much is happening too fast, a characteristic of contemporary US society.

On the one hand, I and my colleagues on the Gordon Commission also worry that speedy action may be addressing the wrong parts of the problem without sufficient information and reflection. Yet, on the other hand, how do we wait and continue to subject children to assessments that we now know are ineffective and suspect may even be impeding their learning? There have been recurring efforts to raise educational standards, with most recent such efforts resuming in 1991. Almost 25 years later, accountability-focused assessment has little to show for itself. We are in a fundamental holding pattern, despite surface changes. Consider that Emily, an 8-year-old is in third grade but once in her life. If she misses a chance to tackle new learning, it will only be harder for her a year or two down the road. Slowing the process down is not what we need. We need a rapid, thoughtful process that focuses on the key issues, rather than one that simply repeats the past with tests that appear different, whose reports look unfamiliar, and whose goal remains to serve bureaucratic needs. Instead we want to progress in palpable ways to affect the real growth of students.

In the northeast (as well as elsewhere), the New York State Board of Regents and the New York Legislature had a heated debate over whether to delay implementation of a new assessment program in New York, in part because the new assessments will likely be challenging and children who have not yet been taught these concepts will not do well. We understand the wish to delay implementation for New York and other states, in part because teachers must be ready and confident to teach. Of course, when expectations change, and children and their teachers have not yet learned to address changes, performance will fall. The drop in performance must be analyzed to determine the elements that are associated with assessment tasks measuring only students' nonschool background experiences and those that can be profitably addressed by revamping instruction, motivation, and materials. Some relevant tasks are discussed in greater detail in chapter 6, where we lay out the model of "dynamic pedagogy" developed by my colleague Eleanor Armour-Thomas and myself (2012).

In the face of resistance to new approaches to assessment, the best way forward is to increase transparency and communications between the many stakeholders in the education of our children. Rather than fearing pushback against the rollout of new policies and practices, we may instead take this as an opportunity to engage parents, educators, and education governance and oversight bodies in a much farther reaching dialogue on how best to prepare our children to live full lives and compete in the global marketplace. What skills and capabilities will they need to be considered as educated in the twenty-first century? How should pedagogy enable them to develop these skills? And, finally, how do we assess whether or not learning is happening—and when it is not, adjust so that it does? These are some of the core concerns we sought to address in our deliberations on the Gordon Commission.

Much of the current public debate on education and its assessment centers on the Common Core State Standards initiative. Certainly, media coverage of the proposed new standards has been rife with misinformation and knee-jerk political reactions. But the truly important debates concerning (1) reform in educational standards and testing practices, (2) the evaluation of teachers, and (3) the high-quality measurement and use of student achievement results should be separated from questions about whether or not the standards movement itself is important or even appropriate. Although these three points are related, they also address our very distinct areas. Much of what is reflected in the Common Core State Standards should be applauded and vigorously embraced. Early rumblings on the rollout of the standards indicate that promising new ideas will be introduced into the usual content of school learning, such as conceptual understanding of both familiar and modern subject knowledge and skills. Some content will need substantial reorganization to take into account emerging understanding and thinking of pedagogical processes. As we proceed further into the twenty-first century, our young people's participation in the labor force—as well as in most forms of political and social life—will depend on their command of certain higher-order abilities. Many of our colleagues on the Gordon Commission and in the education community have praised the Common Core State Standards for seeking to move the education effort toward the development of "deeper learning" skills, which the National Research Council (2012) describes as thinking, problem solving, teamwork, reflection, and communication, as these mental abilities are used in and outside of school. I join them in applauding the values reflected in these new standards. Certainly, they deserve our enthusiastic support and even further development. One way to develop them further is to separate learning processes from outcomes; to that end, I have advanced the concept of "intellective competence," or the metacognitive command of affective, cognitive, and situative processes in order to access, know, understand, interpret, and utilize knowledge and technique. In order to determine if intellective competence is being achieved through schooling, we would look for such abilities as critical literacy and numeracy, mastery not only of knowledge domains but also the kind of thinking that must happen in order for that mastery to occur, analogical reasoning, and the ability to not only conduct analysis but to achieve synthesis—in short, the movement from knowledge to understanding. At this point, we cannot know whether the new standards will enable all students to achieve full intellective competence but they place value on the types of competencies that can indicate that intellective competence has been achieved. After many years of entrenching the education system in practices that value accountability over learning, we can enthusiastically declare that the Common Core State Standards, along with the newly released Next Generation Science Standards (NGSS; 2013), are a definite move in the right direction.

The Gordon Commission consisted of some of the most able scholars and thought leaders in the nation. Among the several issues we on the commission debated, we gave special attention to the new standards and the uses of assessments associated with them. Most members of the commission welcome the direction in which the Common Core State Standards guide us. Few of us are completely comfortable with the current idea that assessments are principally for the purpose of accountability. Instead, we all agree, assessments being developed to measure student achievement of the Common Core State Standards must serve pedagogy well. If they don't, they will need to be revised. Commission members discussed the possibility that modern measurement science provides us with a wide variety of alternatives to the heavy dependence on traditional standardized tests and that the nation would be well advised to explore new assessment strategies. The research and development agenda in the measurement sciences, with a modest bit of time, is capable of providing models that show much greater potential for effectiveness than what can be wisely implemented within the next one or two years. We are aware that only a few of the states have moved very far ahead with experimentation in these directions.

Now, in addition to the research and development work underway in the field, and from very different perspectives, members of the commission have raised a variety of issues that deserve serious examination as we consider the changing relationships between assessment, teaching, and learning. The determination of education and education-assessment policy for the future needs to be informed by some of these issues. As examples, the commission put forth such ideas as the following:

- The major function of assessment in education should be to inform and improve teaching and learning. If we buy into that assertion, the current strength of measurement science—its claim of precise measurement of developed ability—may be impeding students' development of their own capacity to analyze, document, appraise, and understand the processes of teaching and learning. From this perspective, government's role should be to support understanding and improving pedagogical interventions by teachers and students instead of leveraging its total efforts to monitor outcomes and penalize or reward those results. We must study and improve the processes of teaching and especially of learning in addition to the status of achievement.
- Attributions, contexts, perspectives, and situations so greatly influence human behavior that these correlates of human performance must be fully and integrally represented in educational

assessment. This suggestion implies that the validity of data from any significant test may be largely dependent upon these contextual factors. However, since some traditional psychometrics have decontextualized assessment in the interest of objectivity, reliability and validity, and low cost, these factors are often excluded from consideration in the assessment design, development, and reporting processes.

- Traditionally, we have placed an emphasis on student mastery of specific subject-matter content. We suggest that the far more important effort is helping the learner develop the mental abilities and capacities that are both integrated with and the byproducts of one's having mastered such subject matter. The focus of the Common Core State Standards is on such underlying mental abilities—logical reasoning, understanding cause and effect, organizing knowledge, and problem solving—along with mastery of key subject-matter knowledge and principles. Our colleagues advise that questions related to transfer in learning are involved here and should be more productively addressed as we search for the targets of assessment. They are speaking here not only of subject matter but also of changes in the situation or context through which students demonstrate their learning. Transfer tasks are important for two reasons: first, to determine the students' ability to draw from his or her patterns of learning and apply them to new settings; second, to synthesize learning of different tasks, combining elements in order to solve new, innovative, and unforeseen problems. These goals not only reduce the likelihood of cheating or mindless test practice but also challenge traditional notions concerning the primacy of subject-matter mastery as the major goal of education.

- "Dropped-in-from-the-sky," stand-alone tests, decontextualized and standardized, may not produce evidence that is adequate and appropriate to help us draw the inferences that bear on the decisions we must make. The commission considered the advisability of distributed, differentiated systems of assessment, some that occur throughout teaching and learning during the school year. These would be integrated with real-time feedback to learners, teachers, parents, and administrators. Relationally analyzed data from these systems of process- and status-sensitive assessments could thus be used to inform ways to assist learners through adaptation of instruction, designs of new pedagogical interventions, and even administrative decisions. Clearly, this approach requires a renewed and broad confidence in teacher professionalism.

• Some prevailing measurement models are anchored to our traditional commitment to meritocratic values rather than in pursuit of democratic opportunity and do not appear to be sufficiently engaging to or inclusive of students of different backgrounds. It is true that there are questions about the compatibility of functional meritocracy in the service of democratization in societies where opportunity is unequally distributed. This set of ideas may confuse purposes of assessments: those focused on supporting learning, that is, criterion-referenced measures, and those reported in terms of competitive rank, that is, norm-referenced reports. A continued faith in meritocracy complicates decisions to prioritize capacity building as the central function in assessment for education. Nonetheless, meritocracy cannot be shorn from schools if it is widely used to advance careers and further education. The mix must be much more subtle and depends on the centrality of teaching and learning.

In the course of our deliberations, members of the commission realized that measurement science has not been stagnating but has been concerned with much of the advanced thinking around such issues. In fact, there has been a strong movement to integrate the heretofore-separate disciplines of measurement and student learning, so that they are focused on the same desired processes. However, a preoccupation in public policy circles with the important problem of accountability has stalled public education. This focus privileges the measurement of status and neglects the analysis, appraisal, and documentation of the processes of teaching and learning along with the contextual correlates of their effectiveness. This problem area begs for attention as we continue to struggle with the juxtaposition of such values in education as diversity, equity, and excellence in a democratic society.

We may have been much too passive in our acceptance of data from traditional educational testing; we may have been too trusting of analytics that attempt to "prove" the test's validity. In medicine, we use test data primarily for diagnosis and to monitor progress. In education we use test data to select, place, and hold account-able. Modern measurement science is capable of far more. We have models for the use of tests for diagnosis, prediction, instructional sensitivity, and fairness. These models can be adapted to the use of tests to support teaching and learning.

A TROIKA: ASSESSMENT, TEACHING, AND LEARNING

I have advocated for a conception of education as a differenti-ated unity of pedagogy, as a troika of essential, interdependent, and dialectical component processes—assessment, teaching, and learning. The education service institutions of the future would be equally concerned with assessment (not just testing), teaching, and learning. I find it interesting, as I look at the wide variety of activities and programs that constitute the agenda of measurement and assessment, that my pedagogical troika is represented there, still dominated by a concern with testing, but progressively more inclusive of concerns for assessment, teaching, and learning—the primary processes of education. For the future of assessment in education, I predict a continuing presence but less-dominating role for measurement and testing. The field and the institution will become much more deeply involved in teaching as inquiry, inspiration, instruction, mediation, modeling, and assessment (this is the previously mentioned dynamic pedagogy model, which we lay out in chapter 6). The center stage will be occupied by the facilitation of human learning, much of which will be self-directed, independently mediated, and comprehensively accessed from multiple sources. I see the assessment component greatly influ-enced by human judgment grounded in evidentiary reasoning, the disconfirmation of continuously changing inferences, and the relational analysis of data generated from systems of probes distrib-uted throughout assessment, teaching, and learning transactions. I envision a shift away from the assessment *of* education for the purposes of accountability, accreditation, selection, and placement, and toward assessment *for* education through diagnosis, inquiry, instruction, modeling, and mediation for the purpose of informing and improving teaching and learning processes and outcomes.

The Gordon Commission advances a vision of pedagogy—the central mechanism operative in education—that is interactively, dialectically, and transformatively inclusive of assessment, teaching, and learning. Our inclination to make concern for teaching and learning conjoint with the traditional concerns of assessment rests on a vision of teaching and learning as reciprocal human processes, which are directed at the understanding, enablement, and achievement of high levels of intellective competence in all learners. That is, the interconnectedness of assessment, teaching, and learning affords all learners pathways toward the best attachment of information and intention to use it in relation to the contexts in which they are experienced.

The products of these assessment, teaching, and learning endeavors are reflected in the achievement of intellective competence, which references the developed abilities and dispositions to understand as well as to know, to perceive critically, to explore widely, to bring rational order to chaos, to bring knowledge and technique to bear on the solution of problems to test ideas against explicit and considered moral values—as well as empirical evidence—and at the same time, to recognize and create material and abstract relationships between real and imaginary phenomena. These achievements are less focused on what we want learners to know and know how to do and are better aimed at what we want our students to aspire to become, to be disposed toward, and to actually be, that is, thinking, empowered, resilient, and compassionate human beings.

Consider for a moment my conception of pedagogy—assessment, teaching, and learning—as interrelated processes of inquiry; as exercises in the collection of information relevant for understanding human performance; as involving the explication, mediation, and modeling of information; and as the thoughtful engagement with information (knowledge and technique) for the purpose of enhanced understanding to inform action directed at the facilitation of learning and development. There are two implicit moral obligations in this theoretical model. First, there is the moral obligation to seek knowledge and understanding. Intentional human action should be informed. I also consider that we have the moral obligation to act on the basis of one's informed understanding. Education is one domain of human activity in which this moral imperative is essential. Directed learning and development demands guidance from the best and most complete information available.

In addition, let us not forget that the best instruction relies on *both* the teacher's and the learner's understanding of where a student is on a learning progression and the teachers' ability to probe for misunderstandings and to provide guidance toward next steps. Here, I'd like to emphasize that both the teachers' and learners' perspectives are important in determining whether the teaching and learning is happening and if not, why—the subtle point distinguishing this perspective from reforms focused solely on either the teacher or the learner is that the teacher is constantly learning from the learner as well as vice versa and that the two are engaged in a learning transaction. A crucial task for education is to enable teachers and learners to engage with each other better—which means that a crucial task for assessment is to help us understand how best to enable this engagement. Although we have long understood the process of intermittent probing or temperature taking in the course of a learning transaction to in fact be the definition of good instruction, in more recent years, certain scholars like Calfee, Wilson, Flannery, and Kapinus (2014), whose work we will discuss in chapter 6, have extracted this type of probing from the informal teaching and learning rhythm and given it a special name and place: "formative assessment." The emphasis on testing and assessment has given rise to the culling of formative assessment from the rest of the instructional and learning process so that finding out how students are doing and helping them in the course of instruction have greater policy value in a "testing" society. Whether this is an advance in the minds of teachers is not known, but in the commission's final technical report, it was clearly asserted, "Assessment is best structured as a coordinated system focused on the collection of evidence…that can be used to inform and improve the processes and outcomes of teaching and learning."

Clearly, measurement science is capable of serving teaching and learning better than we have. We have permitted the nation to focus on less than the most productive purposes of assessment in education. Using punishment and reward approach in accountability is proving to be disastrous as national education policy. A casual review indicates that measurement science using existing tools is capable of mounting an active program of "Assessment *for* Education." Such a program includes the following:

- Determination of status and learning progression
- Analysis, documentation, and understanding of teaching and learning processes
- Sensitivity to relations between context, perspective, and human performance
- Development of differentiated forms of probes, which are distributed throughout the teaching and learning process

The imperative for a different approach to assessment—one that focuses on assessment of the processes of teaching and learning, embedded in instruction and that encourages cognitive development—is demanded by the rapidly evolving world in which students are expected to function. In order to succeed in today's marketplace—and indeed, to have a fully actualized life—students need to develop skills far beyond subject-matter mastery. The challenge is how to stimulate those teachers who still need to embrace the goals, mission, skill sets, and knowledge required for them to help their students to succeed.

If the intent in assessment in education is to inform and improve teaching and learning, the moral obligation is to generate, interpret, and make available the relevant evidence that is necessary for intervention as action. As Einstein so eloquently said, "Those who have the privilege to know have the duty to act."

BIBLIOGRAPHY

Armour-Thomas, E., & Gordon, Edmund W. (2012). *Toward an understanding of assessment as a dynamic component of pedagogy*. Princeton, NJ: Educational Testing Service. http://www.gordoncommission. org/rsc/pdf/armour_thomas_gordon_understanding_assessment.pdf

Bell, J. C. (1912). Recent literature on the Binet Tests. *Journal of Educational Psychology*, 3, 101–110, cited in G. Giordano (2005), *How testing came to dominate American schools: A history of educational assessment*. New York: Peter Lang, p. 18.

Binet, A. a. S. T. (1916). *The development of intelligence in children (the Binet-Simon scale)*. E. Kite (Trans.). Baltimore, MD: Williams & Wilkins.

Brigham, C. C. (1923). *A study of American intelligence*. Princeton, NJ: Princeton University Press; see N. Lemann (1999), *The secret history of the American meritocracy*. New York: Farrar, Straus & Giroux, pp. 29–32.

Calfee, R., Wilson, K. M., Flannery, B., & Kapinus, B. A. (2014). Formative assessment for the Common Core Literacy Standards. *Teachers College Record*, *116* (11), 1–32.

Chapman, P. D. (1988). *Schools as sorters: Lewis M. Terman, applied psychology, and the intelligence testing movement, 1890–1930*. New York: New York University Press, pp. 22–24, 28, 32.

Coleman, J., et al. (1966). *Equality of educational opportunity*. Washington, DC: Government Printing Office.

Cremin, L. (1975/2007). Public education and the education of the public. *Teachers College Record*, *109* (7), 1545–1558.

Dewey, J. (1897/1959). My pedagogic creed. In M. Dworkin (Ed.), *Dewey on education* (pp. 19–32). New York: Teachers College Press.

Gordon, Edmund W. (2013). A history of the assessment of education and a future history of assessment for education. In Edmund W. Gordon et al., *To assess, to teach, to learn: A vision for the future of assessment: Technical report* (pp. 33–35). Princeton, NJ: Educational Testing Service. http://gordoncommission.org/rsc/pdfs/gordon_commission_technical_report.pdf

Gordon, Edmund W. (1970). Toward a qualitative approach to assessment. In *Report of the commission on tests, II. Briefs* (pp. 42–46). New York: College Entrance Examination Board.

Gordon, Edmund W., Bridglall, B. L., & Meroe, A. S. (Eds.). (2005). *Supplementary education: The hidden curriculum of high academic achievement*. Lanham, MD: Rowman & Littlefield Publishers.

Gordon, E. Wyatt, Gordon, Edmund W., Aber, J. L., & Berliner, B. (2012). *Changing paradigms for education: From filling buckets to lighting fires to cultivation of intellective competence*. Princeton, NJ: Educational Testing Service. http://www.gordoncommission.org/rsc/pdf/gordon_gordon_berliner_aber_changing_paradigms_education.pdf

Grant, G. (1973, September). Shaping social policy: The politics of the Coleman report. *Teachers College Record*, *75* (1), 17–54.

Haeussermann, E. (1958). *Developmental potential of preschool children: An evaluation of intellectual, sensory, and emotional functioning*. New York: Grune & Stratton.

Kaestle, C. (2012). *Testing policy in the United States: A historical perspective.* Princeton, NJ: Educational Testing Service. http://www.gordoncommission.org/rsc/pdf/kaestle_testing_policy_us_historical_perspective.pdf

Kaestle, C. (2013). A history of the assessment of education and a future history of assessment for education. In Edmund W. Gordon et al., *To assess, to teach, to learn: A vision for the future of assessment: Technical report* (pp. 24–33). Princeton, NJ: Educational Testing Service. http://gordoncommission.org/rsc/pdfs/gordon_commission_technical_report.pdf

Mann, H. (1846/1957). *The republic and the school: On the education of free men.* Edited with an introduction by L. Cremin. New York: Teachers College Press.

Meeker, M. N. (1965). A procedure relating Stanford-Binet behavior samplings to Guilford's structure of the intellect. *Journal of School Psychology, 3,* 6–36.

National Commission on Excellence in Education. (1983). *A nation at risk. The imperative for education reform.* Washington, DC: US Government Printing Office.

National Research Council. (2012). http://www.nap.edu/catalog/13398/education-for-life-and-work-developing-transferable-knowledge-and-skills

NGSS Lead States. (2013). *Next generation science standards: For states, by states.* Washington, DC: The National Academies Press.

Pellegrino, J. W. (2012). *Education for life and work: Developing transferable knowledge and skills in the 21st century.* Washington, DC: National Academies Press.

Varenne, H. (2012). *Education: Constraints and possibilities in imagining new ways to assess rights, duties and privileges.* Princeton, NJ: Educational Testing Service. http://www.gordoncommission.org/rsc/pdf/varenne_education_constraints_possibilities.pdf

3

ASSESSMENT CAN AND SHOULD INCORPORATE EMERGING TECHNOLOGIES AND EPISTEMOLOGIES TO RESPOND TO CHANGING PARADIGMS IN EDUCATION

The twenty-first century has ushered in a period of considerable flux for education and its assessment. Educational paradigms are shifting in a landscape of social, technological, and epistemological transformation. New scholarship challenges the way we understand how people think and learn, showing us that the context in which individual students learn is integral to how they perform, and that efforts to assess human performance cannot therefore be divorced from human context. Simultaneously, our society has embraced a growing imperative that high-quality education should be made available to all students in our diverse society, an imperative we have embraced for 50 years but are still failing to meet today.

Unfortunately, the Gordon Commission found that assessment has not responded in any meaningful way to these changes—even as educators attempt to account for the internal and external contexts that learners bring with them, assessment continues to follow the dropped-in-from-the-sky model, testing all learners in the same way and out of the contexts in which they live. As we noted in chapter 2, many of us are beginning to acknowledge that the prevailing notions of knowledge and "intelligence" are outdated. Assessment and the measurement sciences must likewise acknowledge that its models and practices are epistemologically out of step. Emerging epistemologies, technologies, and paradigms offer not only an imperative for change to the field of assessment but also powerful ways of making the necessary changes. Still, the first and most necessary change is a shift in how we view assessment itself: from a mechanism by which we measure and sort learners along a status hierarchy to a system by which we can analyze the processes of teaching and learning so that we may improve educational interventions and improve education as a whole for all students. In this chapter, we will see how assessment might respond to and benefit from changing epistemologies, emerging technologies, and new educational paradigms to improve the quality of education for all learners.

PEDAGOGY: A CHANGING PROFESSION

More than a century ago, my father, Edmund Taylor Gordon, graduated from Leonard Medical School, one of the few schools in the country that were dedicated to training freed blacks to practice medicine. Essentially an arts-and-crafts college, the school trained more than four hundred physicians to serve in black communities throughout the southeast before it closed in the early twentieth century. Its closing heralded a profound shift in the way medicine—and in turn medical education—was practiced. This shift was predicated by the Flexner Report, published in 1910 by the Carnegie Foundation, a seminal review of medical education in the United States and Canada, exhorting medical schools to raise admissions standards and adhere to science-based knowledge and methods in their teaching and research. The study of medicine relocated to universities and the practice of medicine changed as the profession became grounded in modern science. The field of education has undergone a similar transformation. Like the practice of medicine in an earlier era, education has historically been more of an art form. Today, training for educators embraces the principles of modern science.

I took my first course in education at Howard University in 1939. Like all other universities where courses in education are taught, the curriculum at Howard has changed drastically from *how to teach* to *what is the enablement of learning, and when and how it occurs.* Not only are students of education expected to understand the disciplines they teach but they must also understand the disciplines that inform teaching and learning processes. The sciences of pedagogy—disciplines such as anthropology, economics, psychology, political science, and sociology, which are sometimes called "learning sciences"—are moving the education profession away from transferring knowledge and skills to students toward enabling in them the capacity to appreciate and understand knowledge and utilize skills. Today, education is concerned with the following:

• Involving learners in the creation of their own knowledge and understanding
• Contextualizing the learning experience and its content
• Cultivating in students critical thinking toward conventional knowledge and perspectives

As we observed in the previous chapter, the privileging of accountability, prediction, and selection based on standardized academic achievement tests is limiting creativity and flexibility in teaching and learning transactions at the very time when pedagogical and societal changes are demanding greater fluidity, more canonical inclusiveness, contextualist and perspectivist thought, and personalized pedagogical engagement directed by the learner. Assessment in education and pedagogical intervention are moving in opposite directions. These are among the perceived problems that led to the creation of the Gordon Commission. We argue that changing conceptions of and practices in education are rendering more traditional approaches to educational assessment obsolete. We believe that changes in the conceptions and practices of education are moving more rapidly than those in educational assessment.

In a 2012 paper I prepared for the Gordon Commission with educational policy analyst (and my son) E. Wyatt Gordon, psychologist John Lawrence Aber, and education expert David Berliner, we identified the following changing paradigms of education in this new century:

1. *Learners as knowledge managers and knowledge producers:* Education is shifting from "filling buckets" to "lighting fires"— in other words, educators are no longer simply content to fill

students' heads with rote information but are seeking to enable them to learn how to learn; to continue learning over their entire lifetimes; and to become enquiring persons who not only use knowledge but persons who also produce and interpret knowledge. The pedagogical challenge will be less concerned with imparting factual knowledge and more concerned with turning learners on to learning and using their mental abilities to solve ordinary and novel problems.

2. *The three R's, meet the five C's*: Reading, wRiting, and aRithmetic will indisputably continue to be essential skills but thought leaders in education like Sir Kenneth Robinson (2006) increasingly point to varying combinations of five C's as essential processes in education: Creativity, Conceptualization, Collaboration, Communication, and Computation. The C's are joining the R's as the ends toward which education is directed. In the twenty-first century, it will become more and more important that students emerge from their education learning to think critically and creatively, reason logically, interpret relationally, and access and create knowledge. The new workplace not only values basic communication skills such as reading and speaking but also finds increasing value in listening and collaborating skills as well as facility in processing information from multiple perspectives. The capacity to recognize and even create relationships between novel and disparate inputs of information will be rewarded in the twenty-first century. In this century, who we consider to be "illiterate" will include not just those who cannot or will not read but also those who cannot navigate the world of digital technology. Computer literacy will be a requirement of economic, educational, and social intercourse but literacy will also mean far more than the ability to do word processing, social networking, and playing electronic games. Digitalization will change the demands and opportunities of modern societies even more rapidly and radically than did industrialization. As a result, the processes of education and the needs of assessment will change quickly.

3. *Reintegrating knowledge*: In the eighteenth, nineteenth, and twentieth centuries, social scientists sought to remove data from

human contexts in the pursuit of precision in measurement and control in experimentation. In the middle of the century, social sciences began to turn to multivariate analysis to study complex phenomena, taking into account the possible impacts of many variables, and early inquiries into dynamic and dialectical interaction began to emerge. If the intent of any given study is to know "facts," it makes sense to continue to isolate variables. But if we seek to understand our world and the relationships between different phenomena and processes in our physical and social world, continuing to experiment, observe, and measure things outside of the contexts in which they have developed and function appears more and more dysfunctional.

Education and its assessment will have to become capable of capturing aspects of context, perspective, and the attributions that participants in the learning enterprise assign to different experiences and subject matter. Knowing and understanding require that those engaged in assessment take context and perspective into consideration. After all, the reason qualitative methods became so prominent at the end of the twentieth century was because we finally understood how inadequately we coped with contexts. Nonetheless, building those sensitivities into the assessment exercise will surely challenge—and even compromise—the precision and efficiency gained by decontextualization in the past.

4. *Reviving the subjective*: In the interest of scientific validity, we have traditionally privileged "objective" knowledge over "subjective" information. We have been taught that human biases and feelings "contaminate" the truth and have spent the better part of the last century trying to control for or contain the variance that an individual's social and psychological situation causes in how he or she sees the world. We have sought to examine an individual's cognitive functions independent of what in fact makes that person an individual. Yet, modern social, psychological, and biological sciences are pressing us to examine or assess human performance with greater respect for the influence of what we in the cognitive and behavioral sciences call affective, emotional, situative and social processes. Despite mounting

evidence in support of the fact that these processes influence the character and the quality of human performance, the primary source of data in educational assessment today remains objective documentation of human performance on tasks that are removed from real-world context, and from the internal context of each learner. In the future, comprehensive and valid pedagogy—assessment, teaching and learning—will have to be more sensitive to subjective phenomena, i.e., to affect, attribution, existential state, emotion, identity, situation, etc.

5. *Rebalancing assessments*: If we want to meet the challenges of the next century, the central priority of assessment in the future must be to inform and improve the learning and teaching processes that enable learning, an argument I laid out in chapter 2. Empirical evidence—and the newer writings of leading psychometricians—does not support the use of educational assessment data for the sole purpose of accountability, and increasingly, educators are coming forward to say that such practices are actually counterproductive to the pedagogic enterprise. Nonetheless, political pressure and short-term thinking allows this inappropriate use of educational assessment data to dominate how we conceive of and practice assessment.

As I observed in chapter 2, we on the Gordon Commission believe that assessment in education can and should inform and improve teaching and learning processes and outcomes, without ignoring the importance of accountability. Whether the two purposes can be served concurrently, and by the same assessment instruments and systems, is one of the most important contemporary questions to be answered.

6. *The "new" functions of learning*: We will very likely continue to create technologies that make work easier and that amplify and expand human abilities. Some of these new technologies, as with artificial intelligence, could change the competencies we prioritize in education, making some of the current competencies more or less important. Or, more likely, they will exacerbate the need for other competencies that we don't have as much knowledge about how to enable, such as agency (which I discuss in chapter 4), disposition, and what the eminent social

theorist Kenneth Gergen (1990) calls relational adjudication, or, the process by which a person discerns and then reconciles contradictory relationships—what he also calls "public judgment." Digital technologies that amplify human ability may make some of our educational tasks easier but they may also create monumental challenges and opportunities for the people who are responsible for assessing, teaching, and learning, particularly since the future demands on our youth will be in as much flux as the schools designed to prepare our youth for work.

7. *Learning as a social process*: Increasingly, scholars in the social sciences are recognizing that human intellect is a social phenomenon that is both produced by and experienced through social interaction and consensus. We observe that teaching and learning are social phenomena as well. Even the learning we do alone benefits from the social interactions we have had before. Electronic games and distance teaching and learning are some examples of the teaching and learning that occur in relative social isolation but that depend on the collective actions of others. Pedagogy of the future will need to reconcile the individual/social paradox of teaching and learning and the implications of this paradox for assessment.

HOW WE CAME TO DECONTEXTUALIZE ASSESSMENT—AND WHY THIS MUST CHANGE

Together with Emily Campbell, in 2012, I prepared a paper for the Gordon Commission discussing how we might reintegrate context into educational assessment. We begin with a history of the effort to remove both learner context and the context of the competencies we wish to assess. We observe that it was a truly a major development in the history of science when the producers and interpreters of human knowledge embraced empirical methodologies. The moment we began to incorporate the scientific method into our ability to use our observations and perceptions to confirm or disconfirm our notions about the world, we freed human scholarship from the limitations of superstition and dogma in science.

But empiricism had many needs—empirical methodology necessitated systematic approaches to developing comparisons across situations and subjects, objectivity in observation and measurement, and decontextualization. Empirical science required precision, reliability, and replicability. Empirical methods became the standard in the search for general principles and truth. It was empiricism that enabled the development of the remarkable achievements of modern science and technology.

Measurement science grew out of this positivist tradition. In the practice of measurement, concern for objectivity, accurate quantification, and reliability were embraced. Decontextualization and control for subjectivity became the norm. Yet, as we have observed, despite a long history of decontextualization in the interest of greater control and precision in measurement science and science in general, the relationship of context and perspective to human performance is increasingly hard to ignore.

Campbell and I proceed from the assumption that we cannot divorce the understanding of human behavior and performance from the context in which they are developed and observed. Much of behavior and its interpretation are influenced by the perspective by which it is informed as well as that by which it is interpreted. Behavior and performance are more than linear. They are both epigenetic and organic phenomena. As such, they must be thought of, observed, assessed, and understood as dialectical, dynamic, fluid, and living phenomena existing in specific contexts and perceived and understood from specific perspectives. Campbell and I advance the notion that assessment, measurement, and the production of knowledge in general will increasingly need to accommodate the inferred interactions between diverse and multiple contexts and perspectives, and the phenomena or subjects being assessed. Our position should be understood as a supplement that can be added to the positivistic tradition in assessment. It must be acknowledged that the positivist tradition has not only its utilities but also its limitations. It is in recognizing the limitations that this effort at reimagining approaches to assessment in education proceeds.

The learning population—and its needs—are changing dramatically worldwide. Declining birthrates challenge countries to maintain educational standards and oversupply of qualified students or graduates can both strain educational capacity and drive economic growth. Multinational corporations and developed countries are seeking workforce across national boundaries, with some countries investing in education infrastructure in countries with high birthrates. Immigration affects jobs at all levels of activity and the ratio of youth to the aged will require new configurations of work. The tighter linkages among workforces emphasize the importance of developing and meeting international educational standards in order to sustain international economies.

Many modern careers create and depend upon new knowledge, and content is undergoing tremendous change, which, in turn, affects the predictability of jobs and career options. Both the school and informal learning requirements of work in the twenty-first century are being drastically impacted by the expansion of knowledge, the globalization of businesses, technological advances, and the interdependencies of technical and service sectors. In order to navigate the demands of both the workplace and society in this century, individuals will have to engage in serious lifelong learning. The relatively simple definitions of twenty-first-century skills offered by some as a substitute for content knowledge are not enough. In the next chapter, we will discuss some ways of understanding what it will mean to be educated in middle of this century. Emerging concepts in social science research and emerging technologies may permit us to evolve assessment to meet the needs of an evolving learner population.

IMPLICATIONS FOR ASSESSMENT FROM EMERGING DEVELOPMENTS IN OTHER DISCIPLINES

In a document prepared to condense and disseminate some of the significant findings of the Gordon Commission, "Assessment, Teaching and Learning," social theorist student of measurement science Ezekiel Dixon-Román (2011) summarized some intriguing developments in the cognitive and measurement sciences, and how they might be applied toward developing adaptive, effective approaches to assessment.

Advances in the Cognitive and Measurement Sciences

Dixon-Román begins by observing, as we have in this chapter, that the cognitive sciences have been advanced quite a bit by research evidence on learning and development from various disciplines, moving beyond traditional perspectives that place emphasis on observable behaviors and toward more nuanced perspectives of learning—such as the cognitive perspective (which focuses on the development of knowledge structures or procedures for reasoning and problem solving) or the situative perspective (which describes behavior in relation to activity or context). These perspectives are not mutually exclusive, he writes, and should be used in interaction with one another in assessment and teaching. The developments that have advanced the cognitive scientists involve what is known about the acquisition of knowledge and the production of understanding. Advancements have been made in the distinction between working and long-term memory and how to move information from one to the other. We also know the importance of metacognition, the role of prior knowledge, and the importance of practice and feedback. Knowledge transfer and the role of the social context are additional, significant factors in pedagogical experiences. All of this information, grounded in research, has become integral in learning and development, which in turn require the design of assessment and teaching to be in that same spirit.

The field of psychometrics has made many advancements in its more than hundred years of existence, particularly in response and alignment to the research and practice demands of psychology and education, states Dixon-Román. Progress in measurement has developed beyond traditional classical test theory methods and factor analytic models to generalizability theory, item response theory, latent class models, unidimensional and multidimensional methods, growth curve models, and change analysis for continuous and categorical outcomes via structural equation or hierarchical linear modeling techniques. The development and increasing methodological acceptance of nonparametric and Bayesian statistical methods (Manly, 1997; Gelman, Carlin, Stern, and Rubin, 2003) in measurement has enabled greater flexibility and improved methods of estimation.

The enhanced methods of psychometrics in conjunction with the advancements in cognitive sciences have contributed to advancements in educational assessment (Mislevy, 2006). Dixon-Román cites the following from Mislevy (2008):

> Assessment is structuring situations that evoke evidence about students' thinking and acting in terms of these patterns. It is an exercise of meaning-making, too: narratives about what students know and can do, in what kinds of situations; narratives cast in some conception of the nature of knowledge, its use, and its acquisition.

Dixon-Román writes that this new understanding of assessment that is grounded in cognitive theory has produced more learning-oriented models, pointing to such models as developmentally ordered progress maps as assessment design methods (i.e., developmental assessments) and cognitive diagnostic methods. Developmental assessments are grounded in theories of the development of knowledge, skill, and understanding, more commonly referred to as progress maps. Interest in cognitive diagnostic information spurred the formation of Tatsuoka's rule-space model (1983); DiBello, Stout, and Roussos's unified model (1995); Bayes Nets, which is based on the underlying theory of Bayesian statistics; conditional probabilities (Almond, 1995); and, relatedly, Mislevy's evidence-centered assessment design (Mislevy, 1994; Mislevy, Steinberg, and Almond, 1999).

The explicit goal, Dixon-Román concludes, must be to develop a comprehensive, coherent, and continuous assessment system that will help create a more equitable system of education—an effective educational system that will contribute to the development of competence in students with diverse characteristics and conditions of life. Here, Dixon-Román is referencing my concept, intellective competence, introduced in the previous chapter and discussed at length in chapter 4, which is a characteristic way of adapting, appreciating, knowing, and understanding the phenomena of human experience through the domains of cognitive, affective, and situative competence. As I mentioned earlier in this chapter, I and many of my colleagues maintain that most people have the potential to be intellectively competent in an appropriate educational system with equity and justice at its core. In order for the field of psychometrics to move systems of education toward this goal, it is necessary to begin to bridge the various dimensions of human development with the contemporary theories of measurement. The various advancements in the merging of the cognitive and measurement sciences are certainly moving the field of psychometrics closer to addressing the construct of intellective competence.

In an evermore diverse society, it is imperative that we implement balanced assessment systems that enable systems of education that better serve the critically important values—diversity, equity and competence. This achievement will require that our systems of both education and assessment make use of all emerging knowledge to enable educational assessment to appropriately inform and improve teaching and learning.

Developments in Science and Technology

The digital revolution has resulted in changes in nearly every area of everyday life. In a paper for the Gordon Commission, John Behrens and Kristen DiCerbo (2012), respectively the vice president and principal research scientist at Pearson's Center for Digital Data, Analytics, and Adaptive Learning, observe that there are three particular aspects of technology that impact how we think about and implement assessment.

1. Computers allow us to extend human abilities. They allow for complex statistical computing, using rules of logic to search, sort, and combine information to create new intelligence.
2. Technology allows us to capture, store, and transmit data or records of experience across time and geography.
3. Technology allows us to represent the world (or new worlds).

The combination of these digital properties opens new possibilities for understanding, exploring, simulating, and recording activity in the world, and this thereby opens possibilities for rethinking assessment and learning activities, they write. They go on to lay out three distinct areas that require an unpacking and reconceptualization of traditional notions of assessment in light of these opportunities and society's new digital situation.

A Shift from an Item Paradigm to an Activity Paradigm
"Item" is a vernacular term that refers to a discrete piece of assessment interaction and data collection, typically in the form of a question or combination of a question and possible answers (as we see in the multiple-choice format). With the digital revolution, write Behrens and DiCerbo, it is now conceivable that we can extract evidence from a variety of work products resulting from a range of activity, including writing essays, configuring computers, and diagnosing patients. This means we can design integrated, complex activities that present interesting problems rather than focusing on what it is possible to score. We can conceptualize an activity as multidimensional from the start and work to understand all data as meaningful, rather than throwing some away as "construct irrelevant." As a result, we also move from thinking about the correctness of a response to a broader consideration of a variety of attributes about a response, including things such as time taken to complete an activity and sequence of actions taken to solve a problem. Mislevy's (Mislevy, 1994; Mislevy, Steinberg, and Almond, 1999) framework of evidence-centered design, mentioned in the previous section of this chapter, allows for more careful linking of activity, evidence, and inference.

A Shift from an Individual Paradigm to a Social Paradigm
The advent of the Internet has brought about a revolution in social communication that has reinforced the concept of the social nature of human activity. What we have long known from our emotional experience, we now see in the output of our daily interactions: emails, media posts, tweets, and collaborative workspaces such as wikis. Historically, note Behrens and DiCerbo, very few assessments allow for collaboration; the prototypical test situation consists of one examinee seated at a desk being told to "keep your eyes on your own paper." However, new technology allows interactions with characters and other students to be scripted, tools available at any particular time to be defined, rules for interaction outlined, and the community around the experience built. Ideally, systems

should honor the student by creating environments that engage students and invite them to participate rather than coerce them into participation.

A Shift from Assessment Isolation to Educational Unification
Technology has the potential to break down the barrier between assessment and instruction. Behrens and DiCerbo pose the question, when students interact with a digital environment during an "instructional" activity, and information from that interaction is captured and used to update models of the students' proficiency, is that instruction or assessment? In many game and simulation environments, the environment is both a learning and assessment environment in which the system is naturally instrumented and the play is not interrupted for assessment purposes.

In the twentieth century, we created artificial environments and sets of tasks that increase (or force) the likelihood of being able to observe a set of activities and sample them for inferential purposes. We call these tests. They require the interruption of normal instruction and are sometimes called "disruptive" or, to use the term we have used throughout this book and in Gordon Commission documents, "drop-in-from-the-sky" testing. Technological limitations on interacting with students, providing experience, and capturing relevant data, especially in the classroom, often lead to dramatic truncation in the goals and aspirations of assessment designers. Sometimes the truncation may even have made its way back to the original conceptual frame of the problem so that the assessment designers did not even consider the target activity they wished to reach but stopped at distal and common formulations that may have severe inferential weaknesses for claims of generalization or transfer. To counter this, Behrens and DiCerbo encourage specification of the claims assessment designers want to make about activity "in the wild." That is, we in the education and assessment enterprise try to understand the claims as contextualized in practice outside of the assessment environment.

In the twenty-first century, activities, records of activities, data extracted from patterns of those records, and the analysis of that data are all increasingly digital. The day-to-day records of our activities are seamlessly recorded in a growing ocean of digital data: whom we talk to, where we are, what we say, the games we play online, what we do with our money, and where we look online. Behrens and DiCerbo refer to this emerging reality as the "Digital Ocean." Even if keystrokes and Internet search histories may not be able to show the complete inner workings of a person's mind, they offer powerful and previously unimagined insights into patterns of behavior, and can enable us to design assessments that are customized, responsive to context, or learn from the learner. Some exciting implications of this Digital Ocean in providing evidentiary data sources for and new targets in assessment are discussed in chapter 5.

Behrens and DiCerbo conclude their paper with the observation that the digital revolution has brought about sweeping changes in the ways we engage in work, entertain ourselves, and interact with each other. The combination of these digital properties, they write, opens new possibilities for understanding, exploring, simulating, and recording activity in the world, and this thereby opens possibilities for rethinking assessment and learning activities. Ultimately, they state that the emerging universality of digital tasks and contexts in the home, workplace, and educational environments will drive changes in assessment. Digitalization will enable assessment designers to think about natural, integrated activities rather than decontextualized items, connected social people rather than isolated individuals, and the integration of information gathering into the process of teaching and learning rather than as a separate isolated event. As the digital instrumentation needed for educational assessment increasingly becomes part of our natural educational, occupational, and social activity, the need for intrusive assessment practices that conflict with learning activities diminishes. Such technologies will also enable self-assessment and temperature taking by individual learners of their own competencies—a capability that will not only enable learners to constantly learn and adapt but will also give them agency over their own learning experience— both of which we have observed learners will need in the twenty-first-century marketplace but which we have not yet figured out how to enable through traditional teaching methods.

How Emerging Concepts and Technologies Can Respond to the Changing Needs of the Learner Population

As we have seen in the previous section, digital technologies offer us promising opportunities to respond to and incorporate into the practice of educational assessment some of the emerging epistemologies that we discussed at the opening of this chapter, epistemologies that may be integral to our efforts to deliver high-quality education to learners with diverse characteristics and life circumstances in our society. In our work on the commission, we also explored how developments in technology, when applied to how we conceptualize and implement assessment, may help us in the education enterprise to prepare learners for the challenges of the twenty-first-century workplace. Gordon commissioner and senior scholar Eva Baker (2012) observes that there are at least three rational approaches to dealing with the unpredictability of job and learning requirements in a changing global context: (1) educational systems must become both operationally and politically agile; (2) assessment should always include tasks that call for transfer or the application of learning to new, unexpected tasks; and (3) learning and assessment should focus on more pervasive skills that could be embedded in different contexts and changing subject matter, directed toward new applications.

Baker then identifies two simple and clear policy actions. The first simple policy step is that transfer must be regularly included as a part of tests or assessments used to measure learning. The second is to investigate the use of cognitive, interpersonal, and intrapersonal skills—which we can understand as a type of interaction we expect to be demonstrated or as constructs with components that interact with one another (e.g., cognition and motivation). If we take seriously the type and speed of change in the world, we need to focus on learnable skills, which may generalize, combine with other sills, or undergird new ways of conceiving or attacking a problem.

Technology, she writes, will determine much of the nature of educational delivery and assessment systems. Unsupervised personal access to knowledge portends a massive and continuing change that will debilitate efforts to maintain control and authority over learning. Games, an activity seemingly far afield of testing and assessment, have evolved to include simultaneous players, complex narratives, realistic graphics, and interactive tasks. How do such games teach strategic thinking and interpersonal skills as well as require problem solving and situation awareness? Other devices monitor and guide physical activity or enable massive numbers of participants to play a single game worldwide. Numerous games are now attempting systematically, rather than incidentally, to affect learning. Imagine if growth curves for downloads applied to achievement measures or sets of expectations developed by industry or higher education?

Games convey how much choice an individual now has in this domain. Web users now expect personalized rather than uniform experiences. Games development history illustrates two lessons for assessment (Scacchi, 2012): assessments will need to change rapidly, take advantage of technology, and meet learners' expectations, and be personalized and fully adapt to the interests, formats, and expectations of individual learners.

In the short term, Baker (2012) predicts that learning through technology will be based on these connected elements: (1) longer tasks involving both independent and collaborative learning; (2) mobile or device-free connections to technology through camera and sensors; (3) use of virtual tools; and (4) automatic ways of modifying difficulty. Classroom and informal sources of learning and assessment must also be blurred, placing increasing responsibility on students but giving them guidance on how to be successful with different requirements. Technology may also assist and record student performances. These developments mean that proximal learning goals and processes will be more personalized than standardized.

She offers four insights related to assessment. First, personalization is the opposite of formal, standardized, and uniform. Second, embedded, automated testing and scoring will save time as well as increase the accuracy and speed of feedback and accumulation of validity evidence for interferences. Third, when testing becomes totally web-hosted, the security of individual performances is at some risk. Fourth, a limitation of technology-based assessment—although probably short term—is test security.

Using technology to assess is neither new (Millman and Outlaw, 1978) nor has it been executed in a fully satisfactory manner, she writes. New technology has allowed "model" to be used in two ways: the design model and the computation model needed to create a particular task. There are empirical questions to be answered about whether the degree of refinement generated by a personalized approach is worth the effort when compared with prestored instructional or assessment options. Whether or not the system should be composed in real time, the data summaries flowing from individuals' and groups' use over time allow the analysis of the impact of numerous variables derived from a combination of student data, using probabilistic methods. The data are also examined from a theory perspective, and the interaction between the bottom-up analyses derived from student databases and the top-down expectations will suggest experimental or on-the-fly modifications that can help resolve disparities in viewpoints.

In this century, writes Baker, learning skills will be embedded in content or multidisciplinary problems. Technology will be used to design, administer, score, store, and report findings to entitled users. Schools and education systems will not be the only source of assessments. Students will make things, not just give answers. And they will be working in more globalized environment.

Starting from where we are and the benchmark of international performance, changes in demography, knowledge expansion, job instability, and technology growth portends many possible assessment futures. The wisest path is to formulate predictions as questions or experiments on such issues as who will be in charge of assessment, self-assessment, transfer and generalization, the integration of assessment into instruction, personalization, technology and automation, new assessment methodologies, neuroscience, the relationship between populist and expert versions of knowledge, and issues of privacy and security. What we should be looking toward is finding strategies by which the future gets better through technology.

The more assessment situations differ from the real-world situations, even if the shared elements match closely, the less we can count on transfer and the weaker the inference from assessment performance will be. It is harder to assess identities, values, and epistemology than it is to assess knowledge and skills, including the so-called higher-order or twenty-first-century skills, such as communication, problem solving, and information literacy. We can anticipate that the strongest evidence of competence in these skills will be most contextualized, and concomitantly, the stronger the evidence the less portable it will be. Rather than trying to assess such capabilities per se, an alternative is to focus assessment on knowledge and skills, but to do so in a way that is consistent with real-world practices and developing identities. Any assessment of intellective competence will by necessity be a contextualized application of the abstract qualities in the definition.

In his paper for the Gordon Commission advancing a postmodern test theory, Mislevy (2012) writes that assessments are sociocultural systems, with powerful effects on people and institutions in the subtle ways they influence other practices. They do not simply measure existing qualities in students and they don't even just shape the development of those qualities. Rather, they cause those qualities to exist and people's lives and practices to adapt to them.

Any assessment is meant to gather information for some actor, for some purpose, under some constraints, and with some resources. Each actor—teacher, higher-level educator, policymaker, employer, admissions officer, and so on—needs information about how educative efforts are faring in order to evaluate them, allocate resources, or plan next steps. To design or evaluate assessment, we must not only consider what tasks to include but how best to provide information to whomever needs it and for whichever purpose.

A one-on-one tutoring session is highly contextualized and highly individualized, with in-the-moment assessments, but a breakthrough in such a session would be unintelligible to an external observer, thus is inadequate as a summary assessment of learning. A classroom quiz is designed to provide feedback to a teacher to shape decisions about subsequent instruction and is less contextualized than a tutoring session. It introduces the notion of standardization.

Because of their implications for assessment arguments, standardization is best understood in terms of aspects of the assessment structures or procedures that are to some degree determined in advance. The information the SAT offers is much sparser than the individualized, contextualized, and extended-over-time body of evidence that goes into grade point averages, but colleges want these scores because they know the provenance of information, despite its limitations.

The Advanced Placement Studio Art portfolio assessment supports feedback loops at two different levels and uses a blend of standardized and nonstandardized features to support its uses. Although the experience is situated and used in daily learning, certain aspects of standardization make central rating possible. The assessment design thus balances support for students' learning, on-site contextualized assessment for student- and classroom-level feedback, and provides summary evaluations that help college personnel evaluating student performance (Mislevy, 2008).

Jim Gee (2010) observes that we trust the design and learning of the video game Halo more than we trust the design and learning of many instructed courses. Understood within the feedback loop metaphor, Halo play offers contextualized assessment moment by moment, in which the game provides the player feedback in the form of consequences and the player provides the game feedback needed to adjust challenges, respond to actions, and monitor progress. However, "completing an algebra course" is not a well-defined term, as there are many experiences called algebra course and they differ in content and activities.

One unproductive kind of cross-talk about assessment, writes Mislevy (2012), is suggesting that a system replace one kind of assessment with another, when the two assessments are designed for feedback loops that support different users, inform different purposes, function at different levels in a system, or assume different contextual information. Good policy cannot result from a decision to replace or reform an existing system without recognizing the feedback loops that are being served or considering how alternatives would replace or obviate their function.

A NEW VISION OF PEDAGOGY

I, along with my colleagues on the Gordon Commission, advance a vision of teaching and learning as reciprocal human processes, which are directed at the understanding, enabling, and development of intellective competence in learners. In this vision, "to teach" is to enliven, enable, and empower learners through a range of orchestrated learning experiences. Where earlier notions of teaching involved the mere transfer of knowledge, skills, and values, this view of pedagogy makes the teaching person a guide, a coach, a mentor, a model, an orchestrator, and a resource person. As I stated early on in this chapter, there is a symbiotic relationship between teaching, learning, and assessment. Although each of these components has an independent history and a separate traditional constituency, they are, perhaps, best viewed as parts of a whole cloth. In earlier eras, we primarily concerned ourselves with the achievement of scholastic aptitudes. Instead, we must focus less on what we want students to know and know how to do and instead, focus on what we want our students to aspire to become, to be disposed toward, and to actually be—that is, thinking, empowered, resilient, and compassionate human beings.

Given the changes in the demographics in the United States, systems of assessment, teaching, and learning that are incapable of addressing the issues of diversity, equity, and academic excellence will simply become marginalized in the twenty-first century. Assessment, teaching, and learning will—out of necessity—have to be appropriate to the diversity in the population that must be served and informative of the teaching and learning processes in which they will be embedded. Taking this and other changes in the contemporary American social fabric into consideration, this chapter introduces readers to the ways in which teaching, learning, and assessment can and do inform one another and how best to capture the relationship between all the three components of pedagogy into a more powerful educational praxis.

BIBLIOGRAPHY

Almond, R. L. (1995). *Graphical belief modeling*. London: Chapman & Hall.

Baker, E. (2012). *Testing in a global future*. Princeton, NJ: Educational Testing Service. http://www.gordoncommission.org/rsc/pdf/baker_testing_global_future.pdf

Behrens, J. T., & DiCerbo, K. E. (2012). *Technological implications for assessment ecosystems: Opportunities for digital technology to advance assessment.* Princeton, NJ: Educational Testing Service. http://www.gordoncommission.org/rsc/pdf/behrens_dicerbo_technological_implications_assessment.pdf

DiBello, L. V., Stout, W. F., & Roussos, L. A. (1995). Unified cognitive/psychometric diagnostic assessment likelihood-based classification techniques. In P. D. Nichols, S. F. Chipman, & R. L. Brennan (Eds.), *Cognitively diagnostic assessment* (pp. 361–390). Hillsdale, NJ: Lawrence Erlbaum Associates.

Dixon-Román, E. J. (2011). Assessment to inform teaching and learning. *Assessment, Teaching, & Learning, 1* (2), 1–8.

Flexner, A. (1910). *Medical education in the United States and Canada bulletin number four (The Flexner Report).* New York: The Carnegie Foundation for the Advancement of Teaching.

Gee, J. P. (2010). Human action and social groups as the natural home of assessment: Thoughts on 21st century learning and assessment. In V. J. Shute & B. J. Becker (Eds.), *Innovative assessment for the 21st century* (pp. 13–40). New York: Springer.

Gelman, A., Carlin, J. B., Stern, H. S., & Rubin, D. B. (2003). *Bayesian data analysis* (2nd ed.). Boca Raton, FL: Chapman & Hall/CRC.

Gergen, K. J. (1990). Social understanding and the inscription of self. In R. A. S. J. W. Stigler, & G. Herdt (Eds.), *Cultural psychology* (pp. 470–606). New York: Cambridge University Press.

Gergen, K., & Dixon-Román, E. J. (2012). *Epistemology in measurement: Paradigms and practices. Part II. Social epistemology and the pragmatics of assessment.* Princeton, NJ: Educational Testing Service. http://www.gordoncommission.org/rsc/pdf/dixonroman_gergen_epistemology_measurement_paradigms_practices_2.pdf

Gordon, Edmund W. (2001, September). *Affirmative development of academic ability. Pedagogical Inquiry and Praxis, 2.* New York: Columbia University, Teachers College, Institute for Urban and Minority Education.

Gordon, Edmund W., & Campbell, E. (2012). *Context and perspective: Implications for assessment in education.* Princeton, NJ: Educational Testing Service. http://www.gordoncommission.org/rsc/pdf/gordon_campbell_implications_assessment_education.pdf

Gordon, E. Wyatt, Gordon, Edmund W., Aber, J. L., & Berliner, D. (2012). *Changing paradigms for education: From filling buckets to lighting fires to cultivation of intellective competence.* Princeton, NJ: Educational Testing Service. http://www.gordoncommission.org/rsc/pdf/gordon_gordon_berliner_aber_changing_paradigms_education.pdf

Manly, B. F. (1997). *Randomization, bootstrap and Monte Carlo methods in biology* (2nd ed.). Boca Raton, FL: Chapman & Hall/CRC.

Millman, J., & Outlaw, W. S. (1978). Testing by computer. *AEDS Journal, 11* (3), 57–72.

Mislevy, R. J. (1994). Evidence and inference in educational-assessment. *Psychometrika, 59* (4), 439–483.

Mislevy, R. J. (2006). Cognitive psychology and educational assessment. In R. L. Brennan (Ed.), *Educational measurement* (4th ed.) (pp. 257–305). Portsmouth, NH: Greenwood Publishing Group.

Mislevy, R. J. (2008). *Some implications of expertise research for educational assessment.* Keynote address at the 34th International Association for Educational Assessment (IAEA) Conference, Cambridge University, September 8. Retrieved May 16, 2011, from http://iaea2008.cambridgeassessment.org.uk/ca/digitalAssets/138340_Mislevy.pdf

Mislevy, R. J. (2012). *Postmodern test theory.* http://www.gordoncommission.org/rsc/pdf/mislevy_postmodern_test_theory.pdf

Mislevy, R. J., Steinberg, L. S., & Almond, R. G. (1999). *Evidence-centered assessment design.* Princeton, NJ: Educational Testing Service. Retrieved May 16, 2011, from http://www.education.umd.edu/EDMS/mislevy/papers/ECD_overview.html

Mislevy, R. J., Steinberg, L. S., & Almond, R. G. (2003). On the structure of educational assessment. *Measurement: Interdisciplinary Research and Perspective, 1* (1), 3–62.

Robinson, K. (2006, February). *Ken Robinson: Do schools kill creativity?* [Video file]. Retrieved from http://www.ted.com/talks/ken_robinson_says_schools_kill_creativity?language=en

Scacchi, W. (Ed.). (2012, July). *The future of research in computer games and virtual worlds: Workshop report* (Tech. Rep. UCI-ISR-12–8). Irvine, CA: University of California, Irvine, Institute for Software Research, University of California, Irvine, Irvine, CA. http://www.isr.uci.edu/tech_reports/UCI-ISR-12-8.pdf

Tatsuoka, K. K. (1983). Rule space: An approach for dealing with misconceptions based on item response theory. *Journal of Educational Measurement, 20,* 345–354.

4

BOTH EDUCATING AND BEING EDUCATED ARE CHANGING IN THE TWENTY-FIRST CENTURY

To meet the demands of a society and workplace in flux, an educated person in the twenty-first century, over the course of his schooling, will need to develop a set of capabilities and competencies that have not previously been demanded of educated people—such as adaptability, confidence in the face of profound economic and psychic uncertainty, and the proclivity to keep mastering new subject matters and technologies over the course of a lifetime. Various members in the Gordon Commission have attempted to advance concepts that account for both the kind of character and "toolkit" that would signify a person as educated in the twenty-first century. In this chapter, we will discuss both Carl Bereiter and Marlene Scardamalia's (2012) concept of "knowledgeability" as well as my own idea of "intellective competence." As I contemplate the common thread between these two concepts—and really, the essence of what we are getting at when we attempt to define "educated"—I keep returning to the idea of human agency. Perhaps what we are saying is that a person with agency is able to become intellectively competent. So, what exactly do we mean by agency?

In a paper I wrote with Ana Mari Cauce (2012) for the Gordon Commission, we observed that we routinely use terms like overachiever and underachiever, or more colloquially and judgmentally we describe some people as lazy or unmotivated and others as can-do or can-make-it-happen. The saying that if you need something done, ask a busy person, likewise comes to mind. In all these cases we seem to be referring to the fact that intelligence, talent, or high capability alone is not enough to lead to accomplishment or success, whether related to academic realms of accomplishment or otherwise. Even a combination of raw talent and an enabling environment does not always translate into accomplishment. Or as Nobel Prize winning economist Amartya Sen has noted, a person "could have a great deal of freedom, without achieving much" (1987, p. 1). In contrast, there are those who achieve greatness in the face of tremendous obstacles or those who are able to drive their more limited talent toward great accomplishment. What makes for the difference between these types of persons has not been well defined or well measured but the construct that seems closest to capturing it is "human agency" and, of course, the disposition to use it. Or, as our more quantitatively oriented colleagues have described human agency, it is the "unexplained variance" once all other personality and environmental factors are accounted for (Hitlin and Elder, 2007, p. 33).

While it is difficult to find much writing or even reference to human agency outside of philosophy prior to the 1980s, there has been a growing interest in the construct both in the psychological and sociological literatures, especially in the works of Albert Bandura (1997, 2001, 2002, 2006) and Glen Elder (Elder, 1994; Hitlin and Elder, 2007). Human agency also figures prominently in the economic and political development literatures, where it fits into a "capabilities" framework, most clearly elaborated in the works of Sen (1985, 1987, 1999) and Sabine Alkire (2002, 2005, 2008). In addition, a very similar notion, that of individual empowerment, has received growing attention especially in the realms of women's rights, healthcare, and workplace/organizational literature (Nussbaum and Sen, 1993; Nussbaum, 2000).

Cauce and I approach the construct of agency in an integrative fashion that fully acknowledges that while the disposition to act in an agentic manner may be, at least in part, a characteristic of the individual, there are contexts that are more or less likely to encourage human agency and/or to provide necessary preconditions for its expression.

One of the three stated missions of the Gordon Commission is to consider our best estimates of what education will become in the twenty-first century and what will be required of the educational assessment enterprise by the middle of this century. In the pursuit of addressing that component of our mission, we explored emerging and anticipated changes in the paradigms that will in turn change the goals and processes of education. As we illustrated in the previous chapter, the field of education is constantly shifting in accordance with changing economic conditions, demographic data, technological advances, and political debates. These drivers change the ways in which politicians and test makers must conceptualize and ultimately construct curriculum and assessment. As a result, an inventory of the ways in which education is shifting and inquiry into the mechanisms that causes these shifts is central to conceptualizing the future of assessment and education. Current education practices must consider the possible ways that future educational systems can meet, address, and reenvision the concept of education into the next 50 years.

Schools are asked to do a lot, and some schools actually attempt to meet all of the demands placed on them. It is clear, however, that schools cannot reliably and validly assess many of the activities in which they engage. They end up assessing only the tip of the iceberg; consequently, there are many parts of schooling that are not visible and not assessed. This chapter attempts to outline the changes in the ways we need to think about education, as well as the possible future conditions these new ways of thinking create, and conceptualizes a future for education and testing that reconciles new realities with assessment practices.

Why Do We Educate?

The educational endeavor is shaped and informed by the goals that we set for our youth. In a 2012 paper I wrote for the Gordon Commission, along with my colleagues E. Wyatt Gordon, John Lawrence Aber, and David Berliner, we observe that the manner in which we choose our goals and the goals that we select have a substantial influence on the outcomes of our educational system. As such, it is important that we clearly detail what we expect our youth to attain through education as they become adults.

There has been some agreement among stakeholders of the educational system about the purpose of education. Rothstein, Jacobsen, and Wilder (2008) conducted a survey of nationwide educators and parents in the United States, which found that both groups had very similar conceptions of what it wanted from the US school system. They valued basic skills foremost followed quite closely by critical thinking. Then, almost equally tied for third place, were the following: developing social skills, developing a work ethic in youth, developing personal responsibility, developing an ability to get along well with others (especially others from different backgrounds), providing vocational, career, and technical education that could qualify youth for skilled employment (that does not require a college degree), providing a foundation for lifelong physical health (including good habits of exercise and nutrition), developing a love of literature and the capacity to participate in and appreciate the musical, visual, and performing arts, and finally developing self-confidence, respect for others, and the ability to resist peer pressure to engage in irresponsible personal behavior. Broader conceptions of the goals of education can help schools to overcome the overextension of programming that naturally occurs when there are numerous goals and limited resources. Many of the specific demands of parents and educators identified by the Rothstein, Jacobson, and Wilder survey can be combined into broader categories. In "Education & Justice: A View from the Back of the Bus," (1999) I proposed that there should be five broad ends of educational outcomes:

1. The individual's ability to know, understand, and appreciate oneself and multiple perspectives concerning the world
2. The attainment of multiple literacies and oralities, like reading, speaking and writing, and quantitative, scientific, and technological literacy
3. The mastery of bodies of knowledge and the capacity to create new knowledge and techniques
4. The ability and disposition to access and manage information in its complexity and its application to solving novel as well as ordinary problems

5. The ability and disposition to use knowledge, values, and thought to recognize and adjudicate relationships among the phenomena of one's experience

Education in its current form cannot account for the majority of these broad ends or the many purposes outlined by Rothstein, Jacobsen, and Wilder (2008). Curriculum, especially as it has been reactively configured in the wake of NCLB, which was passed in 2001 and signed into law in 2002 and requires states to develop assessments of basic skills, has not been able to provide students with these outcomes. Consider the following quote from David Berliner (2010):

> In this era of high-stakes testing students cannot be allowed time in school to follow their interests. The standards define what students should know at different grade levels, and deviation from that plan is considered dangerous because it might result in missing some items on the states high-stakes accountability test. Of course schools never allowed much time for individualized work, but now even the teachers that made some use of problem-based or project-based learning, forms of instruction that could ignite students' interests through a curriculum more personally tailored for an individual, are not allowed to do so. One size of the curriculum is supposed to fit all students. Yet we are reasonably sure that the twenty-first century economy will require from our work force a broad set of skills, not a narrow one. Thus diversity in the outcomes of the educational system ought to be a goal of American education, not sameness. Education for a Volatile, Uncertain, Complex, and Ambiguous future world, a VUCA world, would seem to demand breadth of talent in society so at least some of the talents that exist in society would be appropriate to whatever the world brings our way. It is like evolution. If characteristics of the niche that one inhabits change, only organisms that are adaptive will survive. This means that in changeable times variation in talents, like variation in genes, is needed. Identical skills, like identical genes may prove of no value for survival. The emerging VUCA world of the twenty-first century, more than ever before in our history as a nation, requires breadth of talent so that we might posses an adaptable work force. The behaviors associated with high-stakes testing work against that goal.

It also is important to consider the purposes of socialization and citizenship when discussing the goals of education. Creating informed and thoughtful citizens that are able to contribute to society is a primary function of the education system. As Franklin D. Roosevelt (1938) famously declared,

> Democracy cannot succeed unless those who express their choice are prepared to choose wisely. The real safeguard of democracy, therefore, is education.

Democratic structures necessitate that participants in the democracy are informed or have the ability to be informed on a wide range of topics. Education's ability to perform this function is telling of how well the system will work and how well the needs of citizens will be met. This goal combined with the purposes and concerns outlined by Gordon, Berliner, Rothstein, Jacobsen, and Wilder allow us to answer our question, "Why do we educate?" To respond to the question we use a definition that is slightly modified from one that Debbie Meier (1994) provides:

> An educated person has the ability and inclination to use knowledge, technique, judgment and imagination in solving the problems that confront them at work and at home, and to participate in the maintenance and further development of our democracy.

INVENTORY OF EMERGING AND ANTICIPATED TWENTY-FIRST-CENTURY CONCERNS

The education enterprise and its processes are very likely to continue to change in the twenty-first century in response to and in incorporation with several concerns, including the following:

- The many major developments in measurement theory and technology over the twentieth century
- Emerging technologies for the amplification of human senses and the capacities of the human mind and body
- The declining necessity of long-term memory and recall in an age of electronic access to and processing of information (short-term, "working" memory remains critical)

- Changing conceptions of the transactions by which teaching and learning proceed
- Growing recognition of the importance of attributional, existential, and transformational processes (see below) to human behavior, consciousness, and intentional performances
- Recognition that all life experiences are educative and productive and should be assessed
- The continuum of knowing, understanding, adjudicating relationships, reconciling contradiction, judging, and acting wisely
- Growing awareness of the roles of context, situation, empathy, compassion, and perspective in human learning, thought, and performance
- Recognizing the tension between using assessments for accountability and using assessments in developing teaching and learning strategies, and emphasizing these latter purposes more
- The growing use of assessments in summative evaluations and their decreasing role in providing information for the improvement of teaching, learning, and formative evaluation

Emerging technologies for the amplification of human senses and the capacities of the human mind and body also promise to shape the future of education. It is not mere science fiction to think about computer chips implanted into the human body making traditional instruction centered on fact memorization obsolete by automating the learning process. Researchers are convinced that cognitive functions can be restored or even enhanced with the use of neural prostheses (Berger et al., 2011). Chemical-induced electrical and magnetic brain stimulus techniques are purported to increase math and writing skills (Naish, 2011). Some predict computer emulation or mind uploading, a process that replicates the exact system of human brain function through the use of a system of computers, can theoretically allow students the ability to recapture authentic thought from the great posthumous thinkers in history. Using a physically preserved human brain, the system can employ technology to reanimate the brain and return it to function without the need for a human body. The process can also seamlessly integrate human brain function with computers and the Internet, rendering personal devices obsolete (Kurzwell, 2005). Computer chips that are structured like the human brain mimic the potential of mind uploading. This technology by itself, without the uploading of human consciousness, can teach us how humans learn through emulation (Takahashi, 2011). In addition, 3D object transport has the potential to provide schools with the ability to "print" physical school supplies such as tables, chairs, rules, pens, and models allowing teachers to focus on teaching and the educational endeavor (Fleming, 2011).

Twenty years ago it was not often predicted that we would all have easy access to the Internet from smart phones, tablets, laptops, and netbooks, all of which have changed the way we think about effective methods of instruction, and these technologies promise to change the ways that we educate. The smart phone, as just one example, gives access to the wiki, making fact retention not obsolete but certainly less important than ever. Take for example the following passage:

> Dickens' Mr. Gradgrind was always a silly person, yet he was close enough to some of the teachers we all encountered to be a recognizable caricature. But in this age of augmented memory and augmented intelligence, the Gradgrinds have to go! Here is Mr. Gradgrind speaking "Now, what I want is, Facts. Teach these boys and girls nothing but Facts. Facts alone are wanted in life. Plant nothing else, and root out everything else. You can only form the minds of reasoning animals upon Facts: nothing else will ever be of any service to them. This is the principle on which I bring up my own children, and this is the principle on which I bring up these children. Stick to Facts, sir!" (Berliner, 2010)

Today Mr. Gradgrind's insistence on facts and memorization seems less and less necessary. Most students in the United States can access facts at any time through Google or any number of search engines. Although low-income, marginalized, or underserved communities often experience lower rates of Internet accessibility and usage, these gaps are closing and are a priority target of funders and investors in education. In a world of constant Internet connection, facts are always a click or two away. The issue, however, is that quick and semipermanent access to needed facts has the power to lessen the ability of students to recall information. In fact, studies show that frequent users of search engines like Google have lower rates of recall of desired information yet higher rates of recall of where to find said information (Carr, 2010; Sparrow, Liu, and Wegner, 2011).

Changing conceptions of the transactions by which teaching and learning proceed alter the way that students interact with education materials. Teaching, at least in some places, and often in those schools serving children of the wealthy, has moved away from the use of the didactic teaching method, which is characterized by direct instruction where students passively receive knowledge (Smerdon, Burkham, and Lee, 1999) to more "facilitatory" (constructivist) methods (Banning, 2005). Traditional lecture is being phased out as the dominant form of teaching in some schools and techniques like the Socratic dialogue, a method of open debate through which participants gain meaningful insight into the topics that are discussed; the experiential teaching method for developing critical thinking and problem-solving skills, in which a person evaluates a recent activity in order to gather information that might be applied toward another activity (Dewey, 1938); and collaborative teaching, which uses groups in order to facilitate learning (Gerlach, 1994) have become more common. These methods challenge students to think and facilitate the learning process rather than engaging students in direct instruction. There is still debate, however, on the effectiveness of constructivist views of teaching. Richard Clark (2009), for example, writes,

> Cognitive architecture places severe restrictions on working-memory capacity and so forced guidance allows students to allocate limited cognitive capacity to learning a successful performance routine without limiting transfer. [Researchers] present consistent evidence from the past half-century where guidance results in significantly more learning than constructing solutions to problems and tasks. (p. 174)

The paradoxical nature of motivation as a characteristic of the learning person, of the teaching person or process, of the community, and of the phenomena that are to be learned have implications for teaching practices, as I observed in my discussion of human agency at the beginning of this chapter. Differences in achievement level between populations cannot be accounted for by a fundamental construct of motivation (Katz, 1967; Banks, 1988). The context in which a student is learning and the history of the student as a learner dictate the student's interaction with the material and his or her ability to achieve. A student's learned method of responding to different assignments and circumstances drives their ability to achieve (Banks, 1988). Additionally, the fact is that we hardly ever foster, under school auspices, the learning in which our children and youth are really interested in. As a result, students lack stimulation and excitement about the educational endeavor. John Deke and Joshua Haimson (2006a) in their report, "Valuing Student Competencies: Which Ones Predict Postsecondary Educational Attainment and Earnings, and for Whom?," found that taking into account the individual strengths and weaknesses of students was the most effective way of deciding which core competencies to improve that would yield the most future success for students. Logically, they concluded that individualized approaches to learning are perhaps the most effective way of ensuring a student's future success. In addition, they concluded that added focus on skills captured by standardized tests might cause teachers to ignore nonacademic capacities—such as work habits, sports skills, leadership skills, prosocial behavior, and locus of control—that are as important to success as skills captured by tests. A second report by Deke and Haimson (2006b) followed 9,977 students from 1988 throughout their academic careers, and sought to identify and observe the skills that were best at predicting achievement in postsecondary institutions. Deke and Haimson found that improvement in nonacademic competencies had the greatest effect on future achievement (Berliner, 2010; Deke and Haimson, 2006b). In essence, what Deke and Haimson unearthed was that national policies aimed at improving the official curriculum areas appeared to not be as effective as local school policies to develop student skills in areas they are already proficient in. Allowing students the chance to develop expertise in whatever areas they are interested in and having teachers teach in their areas of expertise is probably as good as any push to have the official school curriculum running full time (Berliner, 2010).

The work of Deke and Haimson speaks directly to the work of Tiedeman and O'Hara (1963), which asserts that the difference in the concerns of young people are evident when exploring the data that they worry about as opposed to the data that schools worry about. The differentiation between "other people's data and one's personal data" illustrates a conflict between content mastery and activities like social interactions with peers, dating, pursuit of reputation, athletic and social competition, and the adjudication of the relationships in family as well as community politics (Tiedeman and O'Hara, 1963). In the daily life of students each individual must delicately balance his or her own content mastery with his or her own social endeavors. Engagement of students by using ideas and topics that excite them and engagement of the competencies that are particularly strong in each individual, inside and outside of the mastery of core content, should be the focus of schooling in order to better prepare students for future achievement.

As we observed in the previous chapter, the growing recognition of the importance of attributional (referring to the cognitive processes that people undertake to explain why things happen to them), existential, and transformational processes to human behavior, consciousness, and intentional performances promises to change the way we educate. The answer to these "why" questions are framed by self-perceptions that, when recognized, can serve as learning experiences for students (Weiner, 2010). Existentialism's increased prominence in education debates is in large part due to the recent development of situated knowledge and qualitative data. The following quote by Steven Earnshaw (2007) details the connection of existentialism to the changing concerns of education:

> Existentialism is a philosophy that takes as its starting point the individual's existence. Everything that it has to say, and everything that it believes can be said of significance—about the world we inhabit, our feelings, thoughts, knowledge, ethics—stems from this central, founding idea. (p. 1)

According to Earnshaw's definition, if all knowledge stems from an individual's existence then the act of education is a practice grounded in localized knowledge. This idea has important implications for the future of education. Transformative theory is loosely associated with the idea of the person as a knowledge creator. The theory deems the self-interpretation of the senses of learners as significant and the act of interpretation as educational (Mezirow, 1994; Newman, 1994). If knowledge and the understanding of it are dynamic and the learning person is her/himself transformed by the experience of learning, the teaching and learning of static concepts and stable procedures can be problematic.

The push for comprehensive education supported by communities and parents is both an old idea, enshrined in late nineteenth-century progressive thought and in the immigrant schooling movement of the early twentieth century, as well as an emerging concern for thinking about education in the twenty-first century. Thinking comprehensively and relationally about education renders all life experience as educative and productive of what is learned and measured (Gordon, Bridglall, and Meroe, 2005). Schooling can be a productive site of learning through engagement with the right methods but schooling is unable to provide a full educational experience. Therefore, it is important that we do not tie education exclusively to schooling. We need to acknowledge the role of grandmothers, aunts, and uncles; churches, mosques, and synagogues; after-school programs and youth clubs; peer groups and popular cultures; and the like. When communities and parents are engaged, students learn inside and outside of the classroom thereby accelerating their development and making them better-prepared students.

WHAT DOES IT MEAN TO BE AN EDUCATED PERSON IN THE TWENTY-FIRST CENTURY?

In a powerful and insightful paper (2012) for the Gordon Commission, Carl Bereiter and Marlene Scardamalia, cofounders of the Institute for Knowledge Innovation and Technology, ask what it will mean to be an educated person in the middle of the twenty-first century. In order to answer this, they first ask whether such a person would be a different kind of person from his or her twentieth-century counterparts, observing that there are potentially far-reaching behavioral changes resulting from new kinds of social communication. Extreme personalization and fragmentary communication would appear to be antithetical to what quality education has traditionally stood for, they go on to say, but the consequences of a shift toward greater person-centeredness are indefinite at this time. Longer media forms and shorter attention spans may be different manifestations of the same trend—a declining ability to do sustained integrative thinking. Text is gradually being replaced by hypertext and improved media design may make it easier to recover a line of thought but ultimately the challenge is an educational one: to heighten metacognitive awareness, to help students keep cognitive purposes in mind, and to evaluate their current mental states against them. This is one example of the growing educational challenge to promote *sustained work with ideas*, which is also a challenge for educational technology design. Bereiter, Scardamalia and their colleagues are currently working on design of a new digital knowledge-building environment that has person-oriented space for social interaction around ideas, as well as a dedicated level in which ideas abstracted from the social space become objects of inquiry, development, and improvement. This and other project to respond to emerging learning challenges and technological realities century hold great promise for education in the twenty-first century.

In their paper, Carl Bereiter and Marlene Scardamalia (2012) identify two traditional aspects of being educated: academic knowledge and skills, on one hand, and personal qualities, such as character or intellect, on another. Rapid growth of knowledge and the general uncertainty about what the future will demand has raised doubts about the value of knowledge and "hard" skills. The tilt away from academic knowledge is also a tilt away from the things teachers know how to teach with some degree of effectiveness to objectives of questionable teachability. The scope of the term "educated" may be narrowly limited to testable knowledge and skills or expanded to include everything that constitutes being a good citizen but we do not believe it is wise to burden the term with every desirable human quality. Better to acknowledge that there is more to being a good person than being well educated. Eliminating moral perfection from the definition of educated does not mean eliminating moral reasoning but rather frees us to constructively consider the role moral reasoning plays in cognitive processes, alongside knowledge, skills, and aptitudes.

Bereiter and Scardamalia (2012) then offer an evocative distinction between "knowledge" and "knowledgeability." Knowledgeability, or the retention of knowledge in the individual nervous system, has come under scrutiny. A legitimate sub-question to our broader query of what it will mean to be educated is what will it mean to be a *knowledgeable* person in the mid-twenty-first century? They lay out the following criteria for consideration:

- *Twenty-first century subject matter*: Identifying new subject matter has been something curriculum planners have been doing energetically since the 1960s. Identifying what it will take for adequate knowledgeability in the present century calls, however, for more complex analysis. It is not enough to identify topics that are worthy of instruction but rather where schooled knowledge is falling short of emerging needs—such as "financial literacy" beyond mere personal finance but which includes a systematic understanding of economics.

- *Depth of understanding*: Teaching for understanding is widely advocated but when it comes to assessing the depth of understanding, educational assessment does not seem to have progressed significantly beyond Bloom's *Taxonomy* (1956). Depth was operationalized by a hierarchy of increasingly sophisticated things students might do with their knowledge. While it is no doubt true that being able to do increasingly difficult things with knowledge requires increasing depth of understanding, this does not really get at what depth means. Another operationalization option might be to define depth as *what* is understood rather than *how well* the student can demonstrate understanding. New research would have to be undertaken in order to develop an ordered scale of depth of knowledge in all academic domains, such as has been developed in school biology. Defining progressions in depth of understanding is especially challenging for newer subject matter (e.g., probability and systems theory), which lack a history of efforts to identify and teach essential concepts.

- *Quantity of knowledge*: Despite being frequently disparaged in the education literature, sheer quantity of knowledge still matters because it increases the likelihood of making fruitful connections and analogies. Of course, miscellaneous knowledge is not taught but picked up by living an active intellectual life in an information-rich environment. Assessing the quantity of such knowledge presents a problem that occurs whenever students are not expected to learn the same things, which takes on increasing importance as education moves increasingly toward individualization and self-direction.

Building on this concept, Bereiter and Scardamalia note that one obvious implication of the accelerating rate of change is that students—and not just "knowledge workers"—should be prepared to undertake substantial learning efforts later in life. Project-based learning does not commonly have direct bearing on lifelong learning needs. Even explicitly "problem-based" learning offers little experience in dealing with ill-defined, emergent problems students will need to be prepared for. Replacing topic-centered projects with competency-centered projects could probably enliven school experience considerably and be of more direct lifetime value. Of even greater concern is not the ability of individuals but rather institutions to adapt to changing condition, and adaptability at the individual level does not ensure adaptability at higher systemic levels.

- *Cosmopolitism*: Bereiter and Scardamalia use the term "cosmopolitism" to refer to the state of being cosmopolitan rather than "cosmopolitanism," which has come to mean a certain liberal, one-world ideology. As with other human development activities, breaking cosmopolitism down into knowledge, skills, attitudes, and activities seems to miss the essence, which we would describe as "feeling at home in the world."

- *Media literacy*: Students need to recognize the media as (a) causing social change, (b) being shaped by social change, and (c) evolving through the interaction of many factors. More information is becoming available than in the past, along with more varied interpretations of events, but aggressive, sustained inquiry into what is behind the news is being replaced by professional and amateur punditry. The best education can do is help people become their own pundits, which means thinking critically and reflectively about information received. An educated citizen must function as a theory builder rather than merely an opinionator, applying hypothetico-deductive method of proposing and testing a conjecture. It is not just teaching critical thinking or media skills or familiarizing students with new media but engaging students in real theory development about real issues, using new media as a resource.

• *Moral reasoning*: Moral issues have become global and complex, making it increasingly difficult to ignore injustices in distant places or in cultures different from one's own but reasoning about them becomes complicated by issues of cultural hegemony and difference in worldviews. Moral reasoning faces a more uphill struggle than it did in the past, not because of some epidemic of irrationality but because modern communications have greatly increased the persuasive power of visceral appeals to emotion.

• *Rational thought and emotionality*: The new media are elevating means of expression that are alternative to words—a trend that is not necessarily detrimental to rational thought but which poses educational problems if it is accompanied by a reduced ability to follow an extended exposition in text. "Dual process theory" posits two separate systems of response to a single event or message: System 1, an immediate emotional response that typically dominates moral judgment, and System 2, a slower reacting process that provides us with justifications for those reactions. New media are providing both means to provoke massive System 1 reactions and ready-made System 2 justifications for them. System 1 is educable, as in the educating of empathy. Being able to recognize both systems in our judgments and to evaluate and possibly revise them is a new take on what it means to be rational (Stanovich, 2004).

• *Thinking and learning skills*: Education systems treat the need for good thinkers as a skill-learning problem rather than a human-development problem. Because thinking skills tests will predictably and perhaps intentionally lead to teaching for the test, serious attention ought to be given to issues of teachability, transfer, and fairness. The teaching of problem solving demonstrates teachability; it does not offer evidence of fairness or transfer. There is not even adequate empirical and theoretical basis for calling cognitive traits such as creativity, critical thinking, and problem-solving ability skills at all.

Finally, Bereiter and Scardamalia (2012) identify five twenty-first-century competency needs that schools are failing to address adequately:

1. *Knowledge creation*: Producing the necessary knowledge requires not only an increase in the number of people capable of significant knowledge creation but also a citizenry that appreciates it and is willing to support it. Developing students as knowledge creators involves a more radical transformation than understanding theory's role in the advancement of empirical knowledge, one that authentically engages students as participants in a knowledge-creating culture.

2. *Working with abstractions*: A modern worker needs to be able to move flexibly and rationally between concrete reality and its abstractions. Yet applying disciplinary knowledge to practical life has always involved abstraction. Information technology has only made the need to negotiate between the concrete and abstract ubiquitous. Schooling, however, remains wary of abstractness.

3. *Systems thinking*: Substantial theory has developed about complexity and how it evolves, self-organization being a central concept (Kauffman, 1995). An educated person in the mid-twenty-first century will need to understand, live with, and turn to his advantage scientific complexity because of its pervasive significance throughout the natural and social world. Most detrimental ideologies retreat from complexity.

4. *Cognitive persistence*: This includes sustained study and pursuit of understanding, comprehending long texts, following extended lines of thought, and sustained creative effort turning promising initial ideas into fully developed designs, theories, and solutions. Obstacles and distractions from cognitive persistence may be increasing—and both motivational and cognitive issues are involved.

5. *Collective cognitive responsibility*: Collective responsibility characterizes expert teams of all kinds and goes beyond "collaboration." Collective *cognitive* responsibility adds collective responsibility

for understanding what is happening and what needs to be done. Schools can be a good place for developing the ethos and competencies for it, though requiring that teachers turn some of their cognitive responsibility over to the students while ensuring that collaborative activities are cognitively challenging.

Bereiter and Scardamalia (2012) conclude that the assessment of human development necessarily must be done over a time span, typically considering global traits and dispositions. This obviously calls for looking beyond testing programs as we know them today. Teachers are essential to the assessment process not only as observers or evaluators but also as enablers of the kind of activity that is intended to be assessed. This can be extended to many developmental objectives, whether formulated as skills, habits of mind, intellectual virtues, attitudes, or dispositions. In reviewing the five core competencies, discussed above, Bereiter and Scardamalia found that there are well-recognized varieties of *knowledge creation* that fall within the demonstrable capabilities of the young; that the ability to work with *abstractions* may have considerable generality and is dependent on formal education; that there will be effective ways to teach and test widely generalizable *systems thinking abilities* by 2050; that regardless the benefits and detractions of new media, *cognitive persistence* can be improved by requiring students to read a long and complex text and assess their understanding; and that group *collective cognitive responsibility* will need to be assessed at the group level, likely with supportive technology. The kind of change that would make technology truly supportive of educating the mid-twenty-first-century person is a change that places human development goals as central and knowledge, skill, attitude, and other goals subservient.

A VISION OF PEDAGOGY FOR THE TWENTY-FIRST CENTURY AND ITS ASSESSMENT: FROM FILLING BUCKETS TO LIGHTING FIRES

Bereiter and Scardamalia (2012) have eloquently and thoughtfully constructed a framework for how we as scholars and practitioners might understand what "education" and "educated" should be in the next century. For many years, I have been likewise thinking about what an intellectively developed person looks like, and how pedagogy can—and should—enable that development, a concept I call "intellective competence."

One of the greatest challenges in schooling is how to "light fires"—in other words, how to engage students and make them excited about learning. Traditionally, our educational endeavor has been preoccupied with "filling buckets," or teaching students to recall specific content passed on in lecture. Exciting students about learning and education is an integral part of preparing them for future success as students and as members of society. In order to light fires, educators must pay attention to the students' individual capacities, interests, and habits (Egan, 2008).

Along with lighting fires, effective education must seek to improve the effectiveness of assessments. The current state of assessment, teaching, and learning has rendered the already challenging task of engaging student imagination that much more difficult. In its contemporary form, modern assessment does not test for the kind of thinking Egan and other leading thinkers in education scholarship have identified as priorities. One way of inspiring creativity and imagination—and, in turn, student achievement—is to modify assessments so that they include recognition of the contexts in which test takers live. Integrating assessments into the process of teaching and learning, educating with the intention of helping students develop complex, higher-order thinking, and assessing with increasingly diverse content are all strategies that contribute to assessment's effectiveness. As it stands today, assessment in its quest to create and attach value to student achievement stifles some of the very mechanisms that inspire such achievement. It is with this paradox in mind that we turn our attention to the future of assessment and the changing paradigms that will shape it.

The persistent and dominant role that families play in educating and socializing children (Bailyn, 1960; Coleman, 1966; Cremin, 1970, 1980, 1990) perhaps explains the relatively late emergence of schooling in the history of education. But in the twenty-first century, religious institutions, print, and now digital media could overshadow both families and schools as the principal sources of education. With the advent of new digital media, traditional teaching methods—and even teachers themselves—may gradually become obsolete. After all, what purpose can they serve to people who have the ability to inquire, think, produce knowledge, and continually learn on their own? The content and process of study will increasingly come under the control of learner choice and engagement. What will be learned and how it will be learned are more difficult to predict, since the theories that inform education continue to change and learner choice and engagement depend so heavily on the epistemological and political contexts that shape those education-molding philosophies. The gradual emergence of what we can call "autonomous learners" will bring us closer to what John Dewey once envisioned when he famously said, "Since there is no single set of abilities running throughout human nature, there is no single curriculum which all should undergo. Rather, the schools should teach everything that anyone is interested in learning."

The integration of assessment, teaching, and learning as symbiotic pedagogical processes is a necessary paradigm for the future. Assessment has the ability to inform the curriculum for teachers and to reveal what students know or do not know (Pellegrino, Chudowsky, and Glaser, 2001; Pellegrino, 2012). The mastering of specific skills, the discovery of the contexts in which a student can perform these skills, and the definition of the status of a student are the overall goals of assessment. As such, the aim of assessment should be to inform teaching and learning, where the concepts that we assess are developed. Else Haeussermann (1958) wrote about the assessment of developmental potential in preschool children with neurological insults. Haeussermann used descriptive analyses to judge childrens' performance to determine if educational intervention was needed. For Haeussermann the goal of assessment was to determine the degree of difficulty individual children had accomplishing tasks. With this information she could intervene and help them to reach a set objective. Her bidirectional integration of assessment and teaching also proved that descriptive analyses could be used to infer assessment information. Haeussermann's research illuminates the importance of alternatives in the nature and modes of assessment. Herbert Birch (1958) summarizes the situation well, in the following quote, if you place his comments in the context of education.

> The use of a method for intellectual evaluation as an instrument that has positive value for the promotion of training and education is an essential feature of rehabilitation. In this area of work one is far less concerned with predicting whether one given child will achieve success in competition with a group of age-mates drawn from the general population, than with the problem determining the kinds of training and experience that will best promote his own adaptive functional abilities. From this point of view one becomes concerned with the laws of perceptual-motor functioning in a certain seven-year-old child rather than with the question of whether or not he can copy a geometric figure from a model as well as can other children of the same age. In short, the objective of the examination is to provide information about the special circumstances, which are needed to create appropriate conditions for learning in the handicapped child. Such an approach, as Miss Haeussermann so aptly puts it, shifts the "burden of proof from the child who is being examined, to the items which test the level of his comprehension." (p. i)

Dynamic pedagogies, such as the concept Eleanor Armour-Thomas and I developed together (2006), which I discuss in greater detail in chapter 6, use diagnostic test data to create assessments that can identify the cognitive strengths and needs of students. Teaching, learning, and assessment are integrated through the use of curriculum, which guides a teacher's interaction with students. The result is that students are constantly assessed and their assessment leads to personalization of the teaching and learning transactions between themselves and their teachers (Gordon and Armour-Thomas, 2006).

Intellective competence/character is a capacity and disposition to adapt to, appreciate, know, and understand the phenomena of human experience to make sense of the world. We have also come to use the construct to refer to the quality with which affective and cognitive processes come to be applied to one's engagement with quotidian, novel, and specialized problems. Intellective competence/character not only reflects one's habits of mind but it also reflects the quality or goodness of the products of mental functioning. Like social competence it reflects the effectiveness of the application of one's affective, cognitive, and situative processes to the making sense of and addressing the problems of the world. The integration of the core functions of education must develop the intellective capacity of students. The goals of education necessitate pedagogy that instills the appreciations and dispositions needed for the adjudication of values in the service of prosocial needs—needs that support that values of a given community or society. The development of these appreciations and dispositions requires good schooling inside and outside of the classroom (Gordon et al., 2005).

As noted at the beginning of this chapter, human agency is also an important facet of twenty-first-century education. We define human agency as the ability to act in one's own self-interest and the interest of others without being involved in exploitation. Richard deCharms (1977) differentiates between "pawns" and "origins." Pawns, according to deCharms, identify motivation as external and manipulative. Origins identify motivation as internal and integral. Students must be taught to be origins and not pawns or they will refuse instruction and struggle to achieve. Alberta Bandura (2001), cited at the beginning of this chapter, intimates that human agency consists of intentionality, forethought, self-reactiveness, and self-reflectiveness. Accordingly, to be an agent is to intentionally make things happen by one's deliberate actions. But to be able to make things happen one needs to both know and understand what is relevant knowledge and what the facts mean—to whom and under what conditions. Our notion of intellective competence is instrumental in this regard.

Improving mental processes like accessing information; problem/situation perception; analysis and synthesis; logical reasoning; relational adjudication; selective comparison; metacognition and meta-compositional management; valuing and deciding; and human agency should be goals of the educational endeavor. Expertise in a subject or on a topic requires a deep base of knowledge. Fact bases are not enough. The following quote from Beatrice Bridglall (2001) details the creation of experts.

Research comparing the performance of novices and experts in addition to research on learning and transfer, demonstrates that experts are "smart people" who also draw on a richly structured information base. But accessing factual information is not enough. The key to expertise is the mastery of concepts that allows for specialized learning and enables the transformation of a set of facts into usable knowledge. Experts use a conceptual framework to organize information into meaningful patterns that facilitates eventual retrieval for problem solving. And unlike the simple acquisition of factual knowledge, thoroughly understanding concepts facilitates the transfer of learning to new problems. This finding suggests that in-depth coverage of fewer topics that enables learning of key concepts is preferable to the breadth of coverage of subject-related topics. Teachers, consequently, need a substantial knowledge base in a variety of subjects, familiarity with the process of inquiry, an understanding of the relationship between information and the concepts that help organize it in a discipline, and a grasp of the processes in students' conceptual development.

Students who are able to develop their own conceptual frameworks and have the ability to distinguish which situations work best for any given framework are on the road to expertise. Unfortunately, if students are not exposed to this mode of thinking they are less able to make critical choices and to think critically. Students must be engaged in a way that excites them and creates incentive for remembering the constructs that they are taught. Again Bridglall (2001) adds,

> If students' initial understanding is not engaged, they may fail to grasp new concepts and information presented in the classroom, or they may learn the material for purposes of test taking but revert to their preconceptions outside the classroom. Prior understanding in students at any level can impede their ability to learn contradictory ideas unless they are given the chance to explore the errors in their initial beliefs. These facts about learning require that teachers: (1) draw out their students' existing knowledge through creation of classroom tasks and conditions that reveal students' thinking; (2) use it as the foundation for students to further understand the subject matter; and (3) use frequent formative assessments to make students' understandings apparent to themselves, their peers, and their teachers. These assessments are more useful in promoting

learning with understanding than are tests measuring students' ability to repeat facts or demonstrate isolated skills. Schools of education can promote teachers' ability to work with students' preconceptions by helping teachers to: (1) identify predictable preconceptions that make mastery of subject matter challenging, (2) recognize unpredictable preconceptions, and (3) help students to build on their pre-conceptions by challenging them and replacing them when appropriate.

Perhaps the most important competence for students is the capacity to use analytical and logical reasoning. As a result, curriculum that develops the capacity to analyze the world, both quantitatively and qualitatively and to apply logical reasoning to the connections, patterns, and processes in a student's life is very much in need. Social encounters between people may account for much of the learning in these two areas but since the logic of the education may be more conducive to academic experience, the analytics and logic of education may need to be taught to students who have not explored socially.

The problem for assessment is to identify and measure performance indicators that are appropriate to these phenomena. One set of ways to assess the learner's knowledge and skills is to

1. probe their knowledge, skills, and readiness for new learning;
2. check their emerging understanding of new concepts and procedures as well as misconceptions;
3. check whether they have acquired the new knowledge and skills;
4. check how well they are able to demonstrate their knowledge and skills with automaticity
5. check how well they have consolidated their new learning; and
6. probe how well they are able to transfer new learning to other contexts.

Teachers can engage in dynamic assessment (using diagnostic test data to create assessments that can identify the cognitive strengths and needs of students) in which they assess to design instruction that is sensitive to changes in student learning and performance. As such, the primary goal is to provide diagnostic information about students' strengths and weaknesses in relation to the attainment of explicit instructional objectives (Gordon and Armour-Thomas, 2006). In addition, it is thought that assessment should

1. allow for appraisal of discipline-based knowledge of content and procedures, discipline- and situation-based tacit knowledge and metacognitive knowledge, understanding, and skill;
2. be representative of the actual learning experiences and the meta-products of those experiences;
3. probe for progress toward the attainment of discipline-based content knowledge, metacognitive thinking, and learning skills;
4. provide information that informs instruction and learning;
5. use multiple methods, modalities, and formats to appraise learning; and
6. be embedded in the curriculum, teaching, and learning experiences.

As we on the commission concur, and as we have elaborated in chapter 2, teaching, learning, and assessment are dialectical and transactive components of the pedagogical process. They interact symbiotically. Each component is at once separate and part of a whole, where parts are differentially emphasized at various times for different purposes. Once we have identified the appropriate indicators of developed abilities, the processes of assessment, teaching, and learning should be integrated and function dialectically to reciprocally influence and inform intervention. I favor arrangements whereby assessment probes are embedded in the teaching and learning transactions and are controlled by the learning and teaching persons. Those of us who are responsible for using assessment data for purposes of accountability could well be directed to distill from rich records of the assessment-teaching-learning transactions such measurement data as may be needed for that purpose.

BIBLIOGRAPHY

Alkire, S. (2002). *Valuing freedoms: Sen's capability approach and poverty reduction*. Oxford: Oxford University Press.
Alkire, S. (2005). Subjective quantitative studies of human agency. *Social Indicators Research, 74* (1), 217–260.

Alkire, S. (2008). Concepts and measures of agency. In K. Basu & R. Kanbur (Eds.), *Arguments for a better world: Amartya Sen. Volume 1: Ethics, welfare, and measurement* (pp. 355–474). Oxford: Oxford University Press. (Can also be accessed at www.ophi.org.uk.)

Armour-Thomas, E., & Gordon, Edmund W. (2012). *Toward an understanding of assessment as a dynamic component of pedagogy.* Princeton, NJ: Educational Testing Service. http://www.gordoncommission. org/rsc/pdf/armour_thomas_gordon_understanding_assessment.pdf

Bailyn, B. (1960). *Education in the forming of American society.* Chapel Hill, NC: University of North Carolina Press.

Bandura, A. (1997). *Self-efficacy: The exercise of control.* New York, NY: W. H. Freeman & Company.

Bandura, A. (2001). Social cognitive theory: An agentic perspective. *Annual Review of Psychology, 52,* 1–26.

Bandura, A. (2002). Social cognitive theory in cultural context. *Journal of Applied Psychology: An International Review, 51,* 269–290.

Bandura, A. (2006). Toward a psychology of human agency. *Perspectives in Psychological Science, 2,* 164–180.

Banks, W. C. (1988). Achievement in blacks: A case study in cultural diversity in motivation. Human diversity & pedagogy. New Haven, CT: Yale University, Center in Research on Education, Culture and Ethnicity, Institution for Social and Policy Studies, pp. 8.1–8.38.

Banning, M. (2005). Approaches to teaching: Current opinions and related research. *Nurse Education Today, 25* (7), 502–508.

Bereiter, C., & Scardamalia, M. (2012). *What will it mean to be an educated person in the mid-21st century?* Princeton, NJ: Educational Testing Service. http://www.gordoncommission.org/rsc/pdfs/bereiter_scardamalia_what_will_mean_educated_person_century.pdf

Berger, T. W., Hampson, R. E., Song, D., Goonawardena, A., Marmarelis, V. Z., & Deadwyler, S. A. (2011). A cortical neural prosthesis for restoring and enhancing memory. *Journal of Neural Engineering, 8* (4), 1–11.

Berliner, D. (2010). *High-stakes assessments and the narrowing of the outcomes of schooling and students' minds.* Presented at the Keynote paper presented at the "The Blind Assessor: Are We Constraining or Enriching Student Learning?" Symposium, Sydney, Australia. Retrieved from http://sydney.edu.au/education_social_work/professional_learning/teachers/2010/documents/AssessSymp_ProgramOutline.pdf

Birch, H. (1958). Introduction. *Developmental potential of preschool children: An evaluation of intellectual, sensory, and emotional functioning* (pp. ix–xvii). New York: Grune & Stratton.

Bloom, B. S. (Ed.). (1956). *Taxonomy of educational objectives: Handbook 1. Cognitive domain.* New York: David McKay Company, Inc.

Bridglall, B. L. (2001). Research and Practice on How People Learn. *Pedagogical Inquiry and Praxis, 1,* 1–6.

Carr, N. (2010). *The shallows: What the Internet is doing to our brains.* New York: W. W. Norton & Company.

Cauce, A. M., & Gordon, Edmund W. (2012). *Toward the measurement of human agency and the disposition to express it.* Princeton, NJ: Educational Testing Service. http://www.gordoncommission.org/rsc/pdf/cauce_gordon_measurement_human_agency.pdf

Clark, R. E. (2009). How much and what type of guidance is optimal for learning from instruction? In S. Tobias & T. M. Duffy (Eds.), *Constructivist instruction: Success or Failure?* (pp. 158–183). New York: Routledge, Taylor & Francis.

Coleman, J. S. (1966). *Equality of educational opportunity.* Washington, DC: US Government Printing Office.

Cremin, L. (1970). *American education: The colonial experience, 1607–1783.* New York: Harper & Row.

Cremin, L. (1980). *American education: The national experience, 1783–1876.* New York: Harpercollins.

Cremin, L. (1990). *American education: The metropolitan experience, 1876–1980.* New York: Harpercollins.

deCharms, R. (1977). Pawn or origin? Enhancing motivation in disaffected youth. *Educational Leadership,* (March), 444–450.

Deke, J., & Haimson, J. (2006a). *Valuing student competencies: Which ones predict postsecondary educational attainment and earnings, and for whom?* Princeton, NJ: Mathematica Policy Research, Inc.

Deke, J., & Haimson, J. (2006b). Expanding beyond academics: Who benefits and how? *Trends in Education Research,* Issue Brief #2, 1–4.

Dewey, J. (1938). *Experience and education.* New York: Collier Books.

Earnshaw, S. (2007). *Existentialism: A guide for the perplexed.* London: Continuum.

Egan, K. (2008). *The future of education: Reimagining our schools from the ground up.* New Haven, CT: Yale University Press.

Elder, G. H. (1994). Time, human agency, and social change: Perspectives on the life course. *Social Psychology Quarterly, 57,* 4–15.

Fleming, J. (2011, October 18). In a future of 3D printing and graphene, nothing and no-one will be safe from becoming outdated. *Huffington Post.* Retrieved December 5, 2011, from http://www.huffingtonpost.co.uk/john-fleming/in-a-future-of-3dprintin_b_1017194.html

Gerlach, J. M. (1994). Is this collaboration? *New Directions for Teaching and Learning,* (59), 5–14.

Gordon, Edmund W. (1999). *Education & justice: A view from the back of the bus.* New York: Teachers College Press.

Gordon, Edmund W. & Armour-Thomas, E. (2006). *The effects of dynamic pedagogy on the mathematics achievement of ethnic minority students.* Storrs, CT: The National Research Center on the Gifted and Talented, University of Connecticut.

Gordon, Edmund W., Bridglall, B. L., & Meroe, A. S. (2005). *Supplementary education: The hidden curriculum of high academic achievement*. Lanham, MD: Rowman & Littlefield.

Gordon, E. Wyatt, Gordon, Edmund W., Aber, J. L., & Berliner, D. (2012). *Changing paradigms for education: From filling buckets to lighting fires to cultivation of intellective competence*. Princeton, NJ: Educational Testing Service. http://www.gordoncommission.org/rsc/pdf/gordon_gordon_berliner_aber_changing_paradigms_education.pdf

Haeussermann, E. (Ed.). (1958). *Developmental potential of preschool children: An evaluation of intellectual, sensory, and emotional functioning*. New York: Grune & Stratton.

Hitlin, S., & Elder Jr., G. H. (2007). Agency: An empirical model of an abstract concept. In Ross Macmillan (Ed.), *Constructing adulthood: Agency and subjectivity in adolescence and adulthood. Advances in life course research*, Vol. 11 (pp. 33–67). Greenwich, CT: JAI Press.

Katz, I. (1967). *The socialization of academic motivation in minority group children. Nebraska symposium on motivation*, Vol. 15 (pp. 133–191). Lincoln: University of Nebraska Press.

Kauffman, S. (1995). *At home in the universe: The search for laws of self-organization and complexity*. New York: Oxford University Press.

Kurzwell, R. (2005). *The singularity is near: When humans transcend biology*. New York: Viking Press.

Meier, D. (1994, April 16). *Why educate?* Paper presented at the Martin Buskin Memorial Lecture. Presented at the A lecture series of the Education Writer's Association, Seattle, WA.

Mezirow, J. (1994). Understanding transformation theory. *Adult Education Quarterly, 44*(4), 222–244.

Naish, J. (2011, March 28). The electric thinking cap that makes you cleverer…and happier! *Daily Mail*. Retrieved April 2, 2012, from http://www.dailymail.co.uk/health/article-1370897/The-electric-thinking-cap-makescleverer-happier.html

Newman, M. (1994). Response to understanding transformation theory. *Adult Education Quarterly, 44*(4), 236–244.

Nussbaum, M. (2000). *Women and human development: The capabilities approach*. Cambridge: Cambridge University Press.

Nussbaum, M., & Sen, A. (1993). *The quality of life*. Oxford: Oxford University Press.

Pellegrino, J. W. (2012). The design of an assessment system focused on student achievement: A learning sciences perspective on issues of competence, growth, and measurement. In S. Bernholt, K. Neumann, and P. Nentwig (Eds.), *Making it tangible—learning outcomes in science education* (pp. 87–117). Münster: Waxmann.

Pellegrino, J. W., Chudowsky, N., & Glaser, R. (2001). *Knowing what students know: The science and design of educational assessment.* Washington, DC: National Academies Press.

Roosevelt, F. D. (1938, September 27). Message for American Education Week. *The American Presidency Project.* Online by G. Peters & J. T. Woolley. http://www.presidency.ucsb.edu/ws/?pid=15545

Rothstein, R., Jacobson, R., & Wilder, T. (2008). *Grading education: Getting accountability right.* Washington, DC: Economic Policy Institute.

Sen, A. (1985). Well-being, agency, and freedom. The Dewey Lectures 1984. *The Journal of Philosophy, 82,* 169–221.

Sen, A. (1987). The standard of living. In G. Hawthorn (ed.), *The standard of living* (pp. 1–38). Cambridge: Cambridge University Press.

Sen, A. (1999). *Development as freedom.* Oxford: Oxford University Press.

Smerdon, B., Burkham, D., & Lee, V. (1999). Access to constructivist and didactic teaching: Who gets it? Where is it practiced? *Teachers College Record, 101* (1), 5–34.

Sparrow, B., Liu, J., & Wegner, D. M. (2011). Google effects on memory: Cognitive consequences of having information at our fingertips. *Science, 333* (6043), 776–778.

Stanovich, K. E., & West, R. F. (2000). Individual differences in reasoning: Implications for the rationality debate. *Behavioral and Brain Sciences, 23,* 645–665.

Takahashi, D. (2011, August 17). IBM produces first working chips modeled on the human brain. *Venture Beat.* Retrieved December 3, 2011, from http://venturebeat.com/2011/08/17/ibm-cognitive-computing-chips/

Tiedeman, D. V., & O'Hara, R. P. (1963). *Career development: Choice and adjustment.* New York: College Entrance Examination Board.

Weiner, B. (2010). The development of an attribution-based theory of motivation: A history of ideas. *Educational Psychologist, 45,* 28–36.

5

ASSESSMENT REQUIRES REASONING FROM EVIDENCE

As long ago and far away as seventh-century China, standardized tests were used to inform and bolster the judgment of decision makers in selecting who should be allowed to join the imperial civil service. Even in this earliest of assessments, it was the mastery of a seemingly arbitrary skill set—the rote memorization of over 400,000 Confucian characters—that served as "evidence" of the applicant's potential to succeed in a future job. For many centuries and all over the world, only persons of noble or otherwise elite birth had the opportunity to pursue a life of the mind or enter the halls of power, but since the academy has sought to make education a more democratically inclusive enterprise, assessments have moved toward measuring whether a person has developed those abilities presumed to have enabled prior academic success or to indicate academic aptitude. Even though there has been a shift in which developed abilities are privileged as selection criteria, the underlying process has served the same purpose: the process by which human judgment is used to make decisions concerning (1) the inclusion or exclusion of specific persons or (2) the admission or rejection of targeted persons.

When Alfred Binet was asked in 1904 to assist the government of France in distinguishing between those members of an increasingly democratic society who were educable and worthy of the nation's investment in education, a scarce resource at that time, Binet utilized the same process. His test of intelligence was an instrument that measured the extent to which some persons had developed certain abilities, associated with success in the academy, under the assumption that given the opportunity these persons would continue to master the declarative knowledge and procedural skills demanded of them by the institution.

In the selection of civil servants and/or the selection of persons to be admitted to the academy, the decision-making process requires human judgment. In efforts at improving those judgments, and with the rise of democracies, in efforts to reduce subjectivity and increase fairness, those involved in the assessment enterprise turned to the values that seemed to be working in the community of the scientists. As we discussed in chapter 3, the accuracy and precision on which the scientists depended came to be associated with the systematicity and standardization of measures and procedures. If the judgments and conclusions of science were to be considered valid and thus fair, the evidence—and the procedures by which the evidence was produced—needed to be considered consistent across instances and situations. Systemization and standardization were necessary to the validation of the evidence and it was the validity of the evidence that legitimatized the human decisions and judgments.

Both human judgment and assessment require reasoning from evidence. How does evidential reasoning pertain to educational assessment? To paraphrase the definitions included in the Common Core State Standards, the process of educational assessment is to synthesize data from multiple disparate sources of evidential information to make claims about the knowledge, skills, attitudes, and beliefs of students as individuals or aggregated groups. The score interpretation or assessment purpose is the claim, the data is the student behavior, and the warrant and backing are additional information about the item and the behavior of the student (e.g., existing research and theory about item performance and student cognition). It seems clear that by definition alone, an assessment is a form of an evidential argument.

Assessment is not just about measurement, it is about enabling human judgment. If what we are attempting to do in the assessment enterprise is to improve and substantiate the judgment and quality of decision making by educators and school administrators, then assessment must move beyond measurement and even beyond the qualitative analysis of measurement data (a process I will discuss in chapter 7);

it must be applied toward the integration and synthesis of the different sources of information used in making a decision. Evidentiary reasoning—the effort to identify, define, and make use of different sources of evidence that can be obtained from assessment—can be a powerful tool in this endeavor. In a 2003 paper introducing his concept of evidence-centered design (ECD), Mislevy wrote,

> Advances in evidentiary reasoning and in statistical modeling allow us to bring probability-based reasoning to bear on the problems of modeling and uncertainty that arise naturally in all assessments. These advances extend the principles upon which familiar test theory is grounded, to more varied and complex inferences from more complex data.

In this chapter, we will discuss the ways in which evidentiary reasoning—or reasoning from evidence—can and should be at the core of measurement science, and in educational assessments.

FRAMEWORKS FOR UNDERSTANDING THE INTENTION AND PURPOSES OF ASSESSMENT

If we see assessment as an evidence-gathering enterprise, it might, first, be valuable to establish the purpose, objective, and intentions of assessment; walk back from there to determine what evidence is needed to support those purposes; and finally, identify sources of that evidence. In a 2012 paper for the Gordon Commission, Andrew Ho discusses the purposes of assessment laid out by Haertel and Herman (2005); in Haertel's (2012) address at the National Council on Measurement in Education; in Pellegrino, Chudowski, and Glaser's (2001) National Research Council (NRC) report on assessment, *Knowing What Students Know*; and in Kane's (2006) chapter on validation. Ho observes that the number of purposes these leading scholars have enumerated result from a negotiation between parsimony in presentation and accuracy in description, and points out that categories for assessment purposes are neither mutually exclusive nor exhaustive.

Haertel and Herman (2005) wrote that two broad purposes that have perennially motivated interpretive arguments are assessment for individual placement and selection and assessment to improve the quality of education. Stating that their narrative can be read as the rise and fall of the salience of assessment purposes, Ho (2012) writes that their chronology elucidates a transition in the purpose of assessment from measurement to influence. In his 2012 address, Haertel went on to identify seven purposes of assessment: student placement and selection; improvement of educational quality; evaluation of policies and programs; focusing the system; shaping public perception; educational management (the measurement of teachers and school administrators for making decisions about schools); and directing student effort. These intended purposes, he is careful to point out, have had unintended consequences, such as test-score inflation. In their 2001 NRC Report, Pellegrino, Chudowski, Glaser, and their committee identified three purposes of assessment: assist learning (they are speaking here of in-classroom or formative assessment, in which the intended audience of assessment results are teachers and students); individual achievement (summative assessment, comprising such assessments as end-of-year grades or large-scale standardized tests); and program evaluation (any assessments involving aggregate scores, from small-scale research endeavors to international comparative rankings). In his 2006 chapter in the book *Educational Measurement*, Kane framed his interpretive argument as having at least four stages: scoring, generalization, extrapolation, and finally an interpretation, decision, implication, or action. In Kane's illustrations of this interpretive argument in format, Ho identifies a drift of purpose from trait identification and theory development to program evaluation.

In his paper, Ho (2012) explicitly observes the tendency of modern assessments toward a kind of *purpose drift*, noting that the metaphor of *drifting* is not perfect as it implies a passive, glacial process while the actual adoption of new purposes can be strategic, opportunistic, and relatively sudden. Much of the struggle with purpose is captured by the rhetorical difficulty of communicating that validity is not a property of an assessment but a use or interpretation. It is far easier to defend "validity" once, usually in test development, than to exhaustively defend "the validity of uses and interpretations" that are plentiful and require imagination and careful consideration. Ho does not see a danger in drift itself, stating that in many cases it can be entrepreneurial, creative, and a result of or a force for advances in assessment science. However, drift without validation of newly claimed purposes risks unintended consequences.

Fellow Gordon Commission member Johanna Gorin (2012) takes a stronger view: assessment claims speak directly to the intended use of the assessment scores. Gorin thus seems to be underscoring that assessments can only be as valuable as their purposes are clear.

Robert Mislevy, one of the leading scholars in measurement science today, offers a broader lens through which to understand the intentions behind assessment. In a 2012 paper for the Gordon Commission, he describes four metaphors he has used to not only design and use assessments in education but also in his thinking about assessment policy and the potential of assessment:

1. *Assessment as practice*: Within a sociocultural perspective in psychology, a practice is a recurring, organized activity in which people interact with other people and situations. Assessments require some—but not the same—capabilities as the real-world activities for which they are meant to prepare students; and, as a practice occurring in the social world, an assessment shapes the meaning of all the variables in any assessment system.

2. *Assessment as feedback loop*: In this metaphor, we see assessment from the perspective of people in different roles in an assessment system. This metaphor gives us the insight that the value of assessment data is not inherent in either the assessment or the data themselves but depends on who is using it and for what decision.

3. *Assessment as measurement*: Educational measurement is better understood not as literally measuring existing traits but as providing a framework to reason about patterns of information in context. These patterns emerge from the dynamic interactions among students and situations.

4. *Assessment as evidentiary argument*: Evidentiary reasoning provides a coherent framework for extrapolating what students know, are more broadly capable of, and what they should learn next from what they say, do, or make in a limited set of situations.

The "assessment as argument" schema, he writes, connects sociocognitive understanding of assessment as practices situated in social systems with the symbol-system toolkit of measurement, providing a framework for understanding how decontextualized models of measurement acquires situated meaning in context, and how to use it, critique it, and look for instances where the models are inadequate (Messick, 1994). Assessment arguments build on Toulmin's (1958) general schema for arguments.

Gorin (2012) explicitly references Mislevy's model for designing assessments centered on evidence. The argument metaphor, she writes, emphasizes that an argument is made from the knowledge standpoint of some person or group. When information about context is available, the user can incorporate it into her interpretation of performance and have more precise inferences. Standardization is a design strategy that can mitigate alternative explanations, although with counterbalancing costs. A number of tools have begun to appear to help designers craft assessments from first principles using this metaphor, such as the ECD framework proposed in Mislevy, Steinberg, and Almond (2003), which is the strand of research from which the Toulmin schema were developed. This work is proving helpful for developing new forms of assessment, such as simulation- and game-based assessments (e.g., Behrens et al., 2004; Shute, 2011). Design patterns draw on research and experience to suggest a design space for building contextualized assessment tasks around higher-level capabilities, such as design patterns that help construct model-based reasoning assessments in science (Mislevy, Riconscente, and Rutstein, 2009).

Principles of evidential reasoning have often been discussed in the context of educational and psychological measurement with respect to construct validity and validity arguments (Cronbach, 1989; Messick, 1989; Kane, 1992). Mislevy introduced his concept of ECD in 1994, highlighting the importance of evidence throughout the entire assessment design and development process in an assessment design framework. An ECD approach to educational assessment design considers the types of evidence that would ideally be useful to reason about student learning to infer what students know and can do. Assessment is framed as the process of designing observational contexts (i.e., assessment tasks) that provide such evidence in service of some question, claim, or inference.

The ECD framework consists of five layers: domain analysis, domain modeling, conceptual assessment framework, assessment implementation, and assessment delivery. Of these, the conceptual assessment framework is most relevant for discussion of evidentiary reasoning and assessment arguments. The function of ECD, at its core, is to elucidate critical aspects of an assessment to make them more explicit, thereby improving the quality of the assessment argument and ultimately score interpretation and use. It does so by differentiating key subsystems of an assessment related to assessment design, implementation, and delivery. To summarize, Mislevy and Yin (2009) describe the role of ECD as "explicating assessment as evidentiary argument brings out its underlying structure, clarifies the roles of the observable elements and processes, and guides the construction of tasks" (p. 252). By deconstructing the larger complex assessment system into its component parts, more attention is given to some of the assumptions that are often made (with relatively little consideration) when designing and implementing assessments. These underlying assumptions need to be more explicit and understood by users of test data for the evidence to be useful to a variety of users.

Implications of the Evidentiary Argument for Assessment Design and Development Practice

Shifting our perspective on assessment to one predicated on the primacy of evidence has profound implications for educational assessment design and development practice. The strength of any argument lies primarily in the quality of the evidence (i.e., data) and the warrant regarding its relationship to the claim. The quality of the evidence is judged relative to the specific claim; evidence that is persuasive for one claim may not be useful for another. In order to build the strongest argument, one should work backward from the claim by addressing the question, "What evidence would be persuasive of the claim I want to make"? Then ask, "What situation will give rise to such evidence?" The future of educational assessment will be determined by our answers to these questions, answers that may look different from those today for three reasons: (1) changes in the nature of the claims we want to make about students, (2) availability of new data sources that could inform the existing argument, and (3) new analytic tools to translate data into usable evidence that supports or refutes the claim.

New Assessment Claims

A well-formulated evidentiary argument includes only evidence that is relevant to its claim. Data that is informative evidence for one claim may be irrelevant for another. As evidential arguments, our assessments should be designed to carefully elicit that data which serves our evidentiary needs. We must therefore carefully consider whether the claims we want to make from our assessments are in fact those that are supported by current assessments. That is, do our current educational assessments provide evidence about those "things" that we want to know about students?

1. *New constructs*: An informal review of state and national educational assessment systems for accountability reveals a strong emphasis on what some call "basic skills." Though this trend was likely motivated by a desire to improve individuals learning, skill, and overall educational opportunity, the result has been a narrowing of curriculum, a de-emphasis of elective curricula (e.g., performing arts, foreign language), and neglect of critical higher-order reasoning skills that are critical for success in today's society (Crocco and Costigan, 2007). Employers are increasingly dissatisfied with graduating high school and college students' abilities to deal with real-world problem solving and other critical tasks in the workplace (Casner-Lotto, 2006).

2. *Twenty-first-century skills*: In the previous chapter, we have described the unique set of skills currently in demand in the marketplace for educated workers, which have come to be known as twenty-first-century skills, and which we have discussed extensively in chapters 3 and 4. Educators and the educational system are pressed to adapt to these changing needs by refocusing curriculum on these skills rather than more basic skills (Gee, 2010).

As opposed to the traditional curriculum that focuses on highly decontextualized component skills, alternative models of learning and education focus curriculum and assessments on students' ability to apply their "affective, cognitive, and situative processes to solving the problems of living"—whatever those problems may be and whatever processes those require. Gorin refers here to my concept of intellective competence, which I have discussed throughout the book and discussed at length in chapter 4.

3. *New theoretical models*: While a change to the list of assessment constructs has emerged, more for practical and economic reasons, less obvious changes have transpired at the theoretical level with respect to our beliefs about learning that could have equally significant impact on the future of educational assessment design—the differential perspective, the behaviorist perspective, the cognitive perspective, and the situative perspective (the only perspective that considers the individual within a context, rather than in isolation). The focus on interactions between individuals' cognition and the situative context only serves to heighten the importance of task design in the assessment argument. This is a much broader and demanding evidentiary requirement than more traditional cognitive models of learning that focused solely on evidence regarding the "internal" cognition of the individual. In order to capture the necessary evidence to support claims about situated learning and cognition, new evidence sources with appropriately designed context must be developed.

New Evidence Sources

Until recently, what has remained relatively unchanged since the origins of large-scale educational testing is the general approach—sit a student down at a test for a single testing session for a brief period of time, collect responses to a set of relatively decontextualized items, fit a unidimensional model of proficiency, and describe students' ability in terms of performance relative to one another or to some content-related standard. In terms of building an evidential argument, this "drop-in-from-the-sky" approach yields a relatively weak evidentiary foundation for making claims about individuals' ability to reason and function in the world. More likely, evidence from current tests supports claims about a student's ability to use knowledge of a series of basic skills, knowledge of test taking strategies, and motivation to score well on a test (though by reporting a single score, as is typical, we cannot even distinguish the effects of each of these factors on student performance). Claims about student success in higher-education institutions and ultimately in the workplace are only weakly supported by this evidence. This argues for the need of new sources of evidence to be more closely tied to the types of claims employers and policy makers want to make (Silva, 2008). Recent and future assessments that widen the assessment frame to include multiple evidence sources, from varied data, across numerous contexts should provide a more robust argument to support our claims about students' learning and their ability to navigate contemporary society.

While the technological revolution of the twenty-first century has undeniably changed the types of claims we wish to make about students' learning and abilities, technology has had an arguably more dramatic change on the way in which we collect evidence to support those claims. Several types of data provide evidence, connecting data to claims: data concerning students, data concerning the assessment situation, and data concerning students vis-à-vis the assessment situation. Technological innovations have expanded our capabilities to capture student behaviors relevant to all three types of evidence. These innovations can be categorized as follows:

1. *Item types*: Some of the most exciting assessment developments in recent years are those involving innovative assessment tasks and item types, including the use of scenario-based items and simulations. In recent decades the use of performance assessments, specifically constructed-response items in lieu of forced-choice items (i.e., multiple-choice items) increased significantly. Most high-stakes assessment systems now include some form of constructed-response item as part of their tests. This shift has been facilitated by improved technologies that support automated scoring of constructed responses, including automated essay scoring systems. Still, new assessment tasks should

incorporate items that require processing consistent with contemporary models of student learning and cognition (Gee, 2007). Specifically, items and tasks that develop rich contexts within which individuals must reason and respond, similar to real-world cognition, are of interest. Several new task formats offer promising opportunities: scenario-based tasks (which embed traditional test questions into an artificial test context), simulations-based assessments (in which the scenario is designed to mimic the real-world context as closely as possible), and educational games. While both scenario- and simulation-based tasks embed the assessment in context aligned with the assessment claims (e.g., a networking environment for assessing networking skills), some have suggested that the use of unrealistic environments that do not resemble any real-world context may be even more powerful assessment tools—I am referring to the use of educational games as assessments (Gee, 2007, 2010; Shute, 2011). Educational games for instruction are expected to enhance learning by offering a structured learning space in which the complexity, sequencing, and frequency of curricular objectives can be controlled (Gee, 2010). Game interfaces that generate "imaginary worlds" can increase interest and engagement for many school-aged children and, unlike existing assessment contexts, are played out within a social context. As our desired assessment claims expand to include inferences about individuals' intellective competencies, including their ability to strategically navigate real-world social contexts, games as assessments may be our first opportunity to collect the necessary evidence to support our argument.

2. *Novel data sources.* A useful byproduct of technology-enhanced assessments that is equally important for building our evidentiary arguments in future assessment is the data that can be captured and scored, such as data on student interaction with the assessment tasks—the simplest example of which is examinee response time. A rich history exists to support the use of response times as indicators of cognitive abilities (Schnipke and Scrams, 2002; Lee and Chen, 2011). Response times have traditionally provided evidence of processing speed, as opposed to or in relation to

processing accuracy. More recently, interest has shifted to their use as evidence of additional constructs including student motivation and engagement (Wise and DeMars, 2006). Student-computer interactions—such as log-on time, key strokes, mouse clicks, and scrolling—offer sources of complex data that may be captured and examined as potential evidence regarding student learning and knowledge. Little research exists on how log data can be analyzed and scored but the possibilities offer an exciting new evidence source for our assessment arguments. Some research has begun to examine the utility of psycho-sensory data to measure student engagement and attention when learning and being assessed (Sanchez et al., 2011). Physiological measures include pupil dilation, eye movement and fixations, and electromagnetic brain activity; these data have the potential to be more directly part of the assessment argument, not only as part of the validity argument. Considerable research on the backing and warrants for these evidence sources is still needed before operational use is feasible.

So-called big data generated from computer activities and emerging technologies used to capture, analyze, and deploy these data (some of which we discuss in chapter 7) have triggered a number of ethical debates around student privacy and data integrity. Can we legally access and analyze data generated from the online behavior or physiological responses of minors, and can data generated from subconscious or "mindless" activities on keyboards and mouse pads really produce valuable information? Nonetheless, the possibilities of such innovations are compelling and offer a vast new source of evidences that were once beyond the realm of imagination.

THE EVIDENTIARY ARGUMENT FOR ASSESSMENT

At its core, Gorin (2012) writes, an evidentiary argument is defined by the claims it seeks to substantiate or refute. Perhaps the most common criticism of educational tests as the entirety of educational assessment is the narrow focus on the types of claims they can support. The goal of the educational system arguably is not to incrementally increase students' ability to answer isolated questions correctly. Rather, the goal is to capture and understand individuals' capability to interact with one another and their environment in more strategic, adaptive, and successful ways. Educational assessments must reflect this goal. Recent developments in technology, cognitive and learning theory, and measurement and psychometrics have each had unique impact on modern educational assessment. However, assessment as evidentiary reasoning about the claims that interest us in the twenty-first century and beyond requires a more integrated consideration of these related fields. Educational assessment models should parallel our complex cognitive, sociocultural models of learning. The psychometric models should handle multiple types of data and consider parameters that reflect individual and situational factors. The view of assessment as a one-hour, one-day, or one-week scheduled effort must be eradicated. The dynamic processes that should be targeted by educational assessment, if appropriately captured, requires evidence that keeps up with the real-time changes occurring within and around students as they interact with the world. If we are successful in our efforts, then the future of assessment should look more like everyday real-world interactions than our typical notion of an educational test.

The conclusions from the Gordon Commission suggests that assessment is best structured as a coordinated system focused on the collection of relevant evidence that can be used to support various inferences about human competencies. Based on human judgment and interpretation, the evidence and inferences can be used to inform and improve the processes and outcomes of teaching and learning.

The Gordon Commission recognizes a difference between (a) assessment *of* educational outcomes, as is reflected in the use of assessment for accountability and evaluation, and (b) assessment *for* teaching and learning, as is reflected in its use for diagnosis and intervention. In both manifestations the evidence obtained should be valid and fair for those assessed and the results should contribute to the betterment of educational systems and practices. My colleagues and I on the commission maintain that assessment can serve multiple purposes for education. Some purposes require precise measurement of the status of specific characteristics while other purposes require the analysis and documentation of teaching, learning, and developmental processes. In all cases, assessment instruments and procedures should not be used for purposes other than those for which they have been designed and for which appropriate validation evidence has been obtained. Assessment in education will of necessity be used to serve multiple purposes. In these several usages we are challenged to achieve and maintain balance such that a single purpose, such as accountability, does not so dominate practice as to preclude the development and use of assessments for other purposes and/or distort the pursuit of the legitimate goals of education. The field of assessment in education will need to develop theories and models of interactions between contexts and/or situations and human performance to complement extant theories and models of isolated and static psychological constructs, even as the field develops more advanced theories of dialectically interacting and dynamic biosocial behavioral constructs. Emerging developments in the sciences and technologies have the capacity to amplify human abilities such that education for and assessment of capacities like recall, selective comparison, relational identification, computation, and so on will become superfluous, freeing up intellectual energy for the development and refinement of other human capacities, some of which may be at present beyond human recognition.

It is clear from these findings that if measurement science is to be informative of the design and implementation of learning and teaching transactions, it will be necessary to attend to the collection of a broader variety of evidence than have typically been the focus of assessment. Among these are

- the status of the mastery of declarative and procedural knowledge;
- the nature of the learner's command of the mental abilities that have been derived from the process of engaging and learning declarative and procedural knowledge;
- the processes of learning and teaching that are deployed in the pedagogical transactions engaged in by the learner and the time

spent on tasks relevant to the mastery of the objectives of the learning experience; and

• the conditional and contextual correlates of human performance.

Assessment as the systematization and standardization of human judgment requires that we reason logically from evidence derived from appropriate and varied sources. Assessment at its core is a process of evidentiary reasoning concerning inferences we choose to draw from human experience. It is possible, even likely, that broader and better-quality sources of data when utilized in an evidence-based model of assessment may ultimately enable us to avoid purpose drift and the blurring of intentions behind why we assess. After all, good judgment must rest on a solid foundation and we have long held that data is the most concrete form of evidence. For many years, I have been using the term "orchestration" to describe, variously, the processes by which skilled teachers create and manage high-quality learning experiences and by which intellectively competent learners access not only knowledge but also complex processes of cognition they have gleaned through sustained engagement with difficult subject matter in their efforts to master new subject matter and skills. Likewise, a decision maker must orchestrate different types of evidence from different sources in making a judgment about an individual learner, the effectiveness of a classroom or method of instruction, or the success of a single school or entire school system. Like the conductor in an orchestra, the stakeholders in American education cannot simply rely on the skills of individual performers or the track record of past performances; we must stand at the podium, raise our wand, and prepare to engage with every member of our orchestra individually and collectively to make sure that our performance is the best it can be in the century ahead.

BIBLIOGRAPHY

Behrens, J. T., Mislevy, R. J., Bauer, M., Williamson, D. M., & Levy, R. (2004). Introduction to evidence-centered design and lessons learned from its application in a global e-learning program. *International Journal of Testing, 4,* 295–302.

Casner-Lotto, J. (2006). *Are they really ready to work?: Employers' perspectives on the basic knowledge and applied skills of new entrants to the 21st century U.S. workforce.* US: Conference Board.

Crocco, M. S., & Costigan, A. T. (2007). The narrowing of curriculum and pedagogy in the age of accountability: Urban educators speak out. *Urban Education, 42* (6), 512–535.

Cronbach, L. J. (1989). Construct validation after thirty years. In L. J. Cronbach (Ed.), *Intelligence: Measurement, theory, and public policy: Proceedings of a symposium in honor of Lloyd G. Humphreys* (pp. 147–171). Champaign, IL: University of Illinois Press.

Gee, J. P. (2007). Reflections on assessment from a sociocultural-situated perspective. In P. A. Moss (Ed.), *Evidence and decision making* (pp. 362–375). Oxford, UK: Blackwell Publishing.

Gee, J. P. (2010). Human action and social groups as the natural home of assessment: Thoughts on 21st century learning and assessment. In V. J. Shute & B. J. Becker (Eds.), *Innovative assessment for the 21st century: Supporting educational needs* (pp. 13–39). New York: Springer.

Gordon, Edmund W., & Bridglall, B. L. (2007). *Affirmative development: Cultivating academic ability.* Rowman & Littlefield.

Gorin, J. S. (2012). *Assessment as evidential reasoning.* Princeton, NJ: Educational Testing Service. http://www.gordoncommission.org/rsc/pdf/gorin_assessment_evidential_reasoning.pdf

Haertel, E. H. (2012, April). *How is testing supposed to improve schooling?* Paper presented at the Annual Meeting of the National Council on Measurement in Education, Vancouver, Canada.

Haertel, E. H., & Herman, J. L. (2005). A historical perspective on validity arguments for accountability testing. In J. L. Herman & E. H. Haertel (Eds.), *Uses and misuses of data for educational accountability and improvement. The 104th yearbook of the National Society for the Study of Education, part II* (pp. 1–34). Malden, MA: Blackwell.

Ho, A. (2012). *Variety and drift in the functions and purposes of assessment in K-12 education.* Princeton, NJ: Education Testing Service. http://www.gordoncommission.org/rsc/pdf/ho_variety_drift_functions_purposes_assessment_k12.pdf

Kane, M. (1992). An argument-based approach to validation. *Psychological Bulletin, 112,* 527–535.

Kane, M. (2006). Validation. In R. L. Brennan (Ed.), *Educational measurement,* 4th ed. (pp. 17–64). Westport, CT: Praeger.

Kane, T. J., & Staiger, D. O. (2012). *Gathering feedback for teaching: Combining high-quality observations with student surveys and achievement gains.* Measures of Effective Teaching Project. Washington, DC: Bill and Melinda Gates Foundation.

Lee, Y-H., & Chen, H. (2011). A review of recent response-time analyses in educational testing. *Psychological Test and Assessment Modeling, 53,* 359–379.

Messick, S. (1989). Validity. In R. L. Linn (Ed.), *Educational measurement* (3rd ed.) (pp. 13–103). New York: American Council on Education/Macmillan Publishing.

Messick, S. (1994). The interplay of evidence and consequences in the validation of performance assessments. *Educational Researcher, 23* (2), 13–23.

Mislevy, R. J. (1994). Evidence and inference in educational assessment. *Psychometrika, 59,* 439–483.

Mislevy, R. J. (2012). *Four metaphors we need to understand assessment.* Princeton, NJ: The Gordon Commission on the Future of Assessment in Education. http://www.gordoncommission.org/rsc/pdf/mislevy_four_metaphors_understand_assessment.pdf

Mislevy, R. J., Almond, R. G., & Lukas, J. F. (2003). A brief introduction to evidence-centered design. *ETS Research Report Series, 2003*(1), i-29.

Mislevy, R. J., Riconscente, M. M., & Rutstein, D. W. (2009). *Design patterns for assessing model-based reasoning (Large-scale assessment technical report 6).* Menlo Park, CA: SRI International.

Mislevy, R. J., Steinberg, L. S., & Almond, R. G. (2003). A brief introduction to evidence-centered design. Princeton, NJ: Educational Testing Service. https://www.ets.org/Media/Research/pdf/RR-03-16.pdf

Mislevy, R. J., & Yin, C. (2009). If language is a complex adaptive system, what is language assessment. *Language Learning, 59* (1), 249–267.

Pellegrino, J. W., Chudowsky, N., & Glaser, R. (2001). *Knowing what students know: The science and design of educational assessment.* Washington, DC: National Academy Press.

Sanchez, J. G., Christopherson, R., Echeagaray, M. E. C., Gibson, D. C., Atkinson, R. K., & Burleson, W. (2011). *How to Do Multimodal Detection of Affective States?* International Conference on Advanced Learning Technologies (ICALT), 2011, Athens, GA, pp. 654–655.

Schnipke, D. L., & Scrams, D. J. (2002). Exploring issues of examinee behavior: Insights gained from response-time analyses. In C. N. Mills, M. Potenze, J. J. Fremer, & W. Ward (Eds.), *Computer-based testing: Building the foundation for future assessments* (pp. 237–266). Hillsdale, NJ: Lawrence Erlbaum Associates.

Schum, D. A. (2001). *The evidential foundations of probabilistic reasoning.* Evanston, IL: Northwestern University Press.

Shute, V. J. (2011). Stealth assessment in computer-based games to support learning. In S. Tobias & J. D. Fletcher (Eds.), *Computer games and instruction* (pp. 503–524). Charlotte, NC: Information Age Publishing.

Silva, E. (2008). *Measuring skills for the 21st century.* Washington, DC: Education Sector Reports.

Toulmin, S. E. (1958). *The uses of argument.* Cambridge: Cambridge University Press.

Wise, S., & DeMars, C. (2006). An application of item response time: The effort-moderated IRT model. *Journal of Educational Measurement, 43* (1), 19–38.

6

NEW APPROACHES TO ASSESSMENT THAT MOVE IN THE RIGHT DIRECTION

In chapter 2, I advocated for weaving assessment, teaching, and learning into a single cloth. By this, I mean that assessments should not only be interspersed throughout the teaching and learning process but also that they should actually guide the decisions teachers make about how to teach and students make about how to learn. There is a long tradition of using assessments to inform educational interventions. Yet most of these assessments, even those that have been incorporated into teaching and learning, are still assessments of developed ability. Assessments that are backward looking can hardly be expected to help us move the education enterprise forward. By making assessments responsive to newer epistemologies in the cognitive sciences and by availing ourselves of the technologies that would make such assessments less costly and more practical than before, it is possible that we can use assessment in education to guide abilities as they are developing, instead of assessing to determine whether abilities have or have not been developed. The good news is that there are a number of approaches to assessment that are already widely in practice that move in this direction.

In this chapter, we examine the emergence of promising forms of assessment, such as dynamic (or adaptive) assessment or formative assessment, which might serve as building blocks for the kinds of assessment that are really woven into the teaching and learning processes. In their current forms, both formative and dynamic assessments still rely on measurements of developed ability to inform teachers what learners are missing or need, and have not really been used to understand the processes by which they have either achieved or failed. I argue that these assessments can be modified to help us understand these processes—that, rather than inventing new forms of assessment, we can simply shift the targets of existing forms of assessments and in doing so, can gain invaluable insight into how we can improve teaching and learning outcomes in the United States today.

The Gordon Commission maintains that an aligned and developmental design of assessment, curriculum, and pedagogy will enable an equitable system of learning and development. Such alignment is within our grasp. As discussed in chapter 3, scholarship in cognitive psychology and measurement sciences offer us evidence and modes for evaluating and updating both the forms and objectives of assessment and new technologies will enable us to implement these new forms at a lower cost than we believe possible. This chapter serves to illuminate how we may build on existing traditions in assessment, simply by shifting the focus to design an assessment system that meets the needs of all learners in the system.

FROM SUMMATIVE ASSESSMENTS TO FORMATIVE ASSESSMENT

Recent decades have seen considerable advancements in integrating cognitive and measurement sciences and conceptualized assessment into the "formative" and "summative" domains. In an essay for a pamphlet circulated to stakeholders in the Gordon Commission, titled "Assessment to Inform Teaching and Learning," Ezekiel Dixon-Román (2011) succinctly describes and situates these two forms of assessment.

In his 2011 essay, Dixon-Román writes that summative assessments are large-scale assessments that focus on aspects that have been defined as most critical by curriculum standards and have primarily been used in post hoc decision making, such as promotion, accountability, evaluation, and policy, as well as sources of information for parents on their child's progress and for teachers on students' instructional needs. He describes formative assessment as a collection of measurement methods that are embedded in instruction and provide feedback to both the teacher and student on the student's learning and developmental progress. He writes that they have been used to inform instructional strategies; its proponents claim they can be used to assist in the development of a student's metacognitive competence.

Although summative assessments, historically and currently, receive the most research and policy attention, it is formative assessments that offer the most important possibilities for enabling learning in all US students. Formative assessment, which embodies the developmental spirit of Vygotsky (1978) and incorporates cognitive and situative perspectives of learning (Greeno, 1998), can provide feedback to teachers on the skills an individual student has developed, in order to inform the pedagogical strategy and creation of necessary scaffolding. Formative assessments do not have the high stakes associated with summative assessments (which drive decision making) because they are embedded in instruction and performed unobtrusively throughout the instructional period. Formative assessments also do not have the high direct cost that summative assessments carry and have a greater effect on learning. In fact, in a study that Black and Wiliam (1998) conducted examining gains between pretests and posttests, comparing programs that used formative assessment against matched control groups, effect sizes in the range of 0.4 and 0.7 were found. Dixon-Román puts these findings in practical terms, writing that an effect size of 0.7 would raise the US ranking on the Third International Mathematics and Science Study from the middle of the 41 participating countries to one of the top 5.

Although there are various ways of conducting formative assessments—such as in-classroom dialogue, questioning, seatwork and homework assignments, formal tests, less formal quizzes, projects, and portfolios—Dixon-Román emphasizes that the true potential of formative assessment lies not in its format but in the vision informing it. As stated in Pellegrino, Chudowsky, and Glaser's (2001) National Research Council (NRC) report titled, "Knowing What Students Know,"

The development of good formative assessment requires radical changes in the ways students are encouraged to express their ideas and in the ways teachers give feedback to students so they can develop the ability to manage and guide their own learning. (p. 227)

The most helpful type of feedback provides specific comments about errors and suggestions for improvement and encourages students to thoughtfully engage the task rather than provide the right answer. The quality of this feedback can have direct implications for students' academic identity, the classroom culture, ideologies of ability, and affective development. Thus, underlying the effectiveness of formative assessment is the importance of the availability of high-quality professional development.

Further in this chapter, we will summarize the work of Robert Calfee, who offers a complimentary but more comprehensive definition of formative assessment, which incorporates both the objectives and formats of this type of assessment and offers a moving vision of not only what formative assessment has been but what it can be. We will return to Calfee's work in a moment, but before we do, I would like to draw attention to an ongoing research initiative at Educational Testing Services (ETS) called Cognitively Based Assessment of, for, and as Learning (CBAL™), which not only serves as a good example of a formative assessment that might be widely implemented but also indicates that the idea of formative assessment has gained foothold at some of the leading institutions in the educational testing enterprise. Although CBAL, like other formative assessments currently in use, continues to emphasize developed ability, it does move toward analyzing how students think, learn, and develop abilities.

In a paper he prepared for the Gordon Commission, and further developed for inclusion in a special issue of *Teachers College Record*, Randy Bennett, ETS's Norman O. Fredrikson Chair in Assessment Innovation, observes that educators and administrators today require assessments to provide meaningful information for summative and formative purposes—indeed, for multiple summative and multiple formative purposes. Multiple purposes, he writes, might best be served by different, related assessments designed to work in synergistic ways—that is, through modular systems of assessment. Research initiatives such as CBAL, in which he plays a lead role, as well as the Smarter Balanced Assessment Consortium (2010) and Partnership for Assessment of Readiness for College and Careers (2010) assessment consortia, are examples of modular systems of assessment.

Dixon-Román (2011) offers an overview of CBAL, noting that the initiative begins with the premise that K-12 accountability assessments could be markedly improved by incorporating

- findings from learning sciences research about what it means to be proficient in a domain (in addition to Common Core State Standards);
- tasks that model effective teaching and learning practice;
- mechanisms for returning information about student performance in a rapid enough fashion to be of use to teachers and students; and
- testing on multiple occasions so that highly consequential decisions have a stronger evidential basis.

In the CBAL Initiative, he writes, ETS's central goal is to create a future comprehensive system of assessment that

- documents what students have achieved ("of learning");
- helps identify how to plan and adjust instruction ("for learning"); and
- is considered by students and teachers to be a worthwhile educational experience in and of itself ("as learning").

He describes CBAL as a system that attempts to unify and create synergy among accountability testing, formative assessment, instruction, and professional support, with the following key characteristics:

- Accountability tests, formative assessment, and professional support will be derived from the same conceptual base. That base will be built upon cognitive-scientific research, Common Core State Standards and curricular considerations.
- The CBAL assessments will consist largely of engaging, extended, constructed-response tasks that are delivered primarily by computer and, to the extent feasible, automatically scored.

- Because of their nature, the CBAL tasks should be viewed by teachers and students as worthwhile learning experiences in and of themselves. Ideally, taking the test should be an educational experience and preparing for it should have the effect of improving student domain competency, not just improving performance on the test.
- Accountability tests will be distributed over several administrations throughout the school year so that (1) the importance of any one assessment on an occasion is diminished; (2) tasks can be more complex and more integrative because more time is available for assessment in the aggregate; and (3) the assessments provide prompt interim information to teachers while there is time to take instructional action.
- For accountability purposes, estimates of student competency will be aggregations of information collected over time. In addition to these competency estimates, the accountability tests will offer some formative information to teachers, students, parents, and local policymakers.
- Results from the accountability tests will serve as initial information for more extensive formative or diagnostic assessment, indicating such things as the competency level, area(s) in which follow-up is suggested, and initial formative hypotheses. (However, the CBAL formative assessments will never be used for accountability purposes.)

CBAL is one example of a curriculum-embedded assessment. CBAL data are used to inform further instructional development; this is an example of assessment that is embedded in the teaching and learning process, the pedagogical troika I have advocated for much of the last two decades. CBAL offers perhaps the best developed model of assessment that attempts to be both didactic and analytic. Still, implementing even this model of formative assessment as a primary approach to assessment nationwide poses a number of challenges. As Bennett (2014) writes, the operational infrastructure in most large testing programs today can accommodate simple measurement models, generally models that rank examinees along a hierarchy that has a single dimension. The operational infrastructure needs to be created.

In an enormously rich paper on formative assessment prepared for the commission, Calfee, Wilson, Flannery, and Kapinus (2014) quote Haertel's (2014) reflection on the contributions of the Gordon Commission as presenting a more detailed picture of the possibilities of formative assessment to foster learning:

> [In my vision of the future of schooling], classroom assessment will be truly integrated with instruction, based on student pursuits that are educationally useful and intrinsically meaningful in the classroom context. Observations of the processes as well as the products of student learning activities will inform assessment inferences. Records of students' actions will be captured and analyzed to support high-level inferences about their reasoning and expertise.

Calfee and colleagues (2014) also quote McManus as follows: "Formative assessment is a process used by teachers and students during instruction that provides feedback to adjust ongoing teaching and learning to improve student achievement of intended outcomes" (2008, p. 5). McManus expands this definition with several helpful comments:

1. Formative assessment is a process rather than a particular kind of assessment...There is no such thing as a "formative test."
2. The formative assessment process involves both teachers and students...both of whom must be actively involved in the process of improving learning.
3. Learning progressions *(or a plan for how learners should move from where they are to where they need to be, authors)* provide teachers with the big picture of what students need to learn, along with sufficient detail for planning instruction to meet short-term goals. (These progressions are not unlike "scope and sequence" guidance given to teachers in earlier times, authors.)
4. Teachers must provide [students] the criteria by which learning will be assessed...using readily understood language, and realistic examples that meet and do not meet the criteria to advance significantly and to reshape previous conceptions. (McManus, 2008)

This description clarifies, deepens, and expands upon the descriptive and purposive definition offered by Dixon-Román, and captures the main themes and distinctive features of the type of instruction known as formative assessment.

Although formative assessment as conceptualized by Calfee and colleagues offers a brightly lit pathway toward shifting the purposes and targets of assessment toward the development of learners rather than simply measuring the status of learners, it still stays with the tradition in assessment of measuring developed ability. To be informative of intervention, assessment must focus on process instead of status. Assessments must analyze processes; from the data analyzing process we must make diagnostic inferences, from which we can make prescriptive inferences, so that ultimately we intervene didactically to both examine and to instruct. Formative assessment offers the best current approach to achieving this vision of assessment, but in order to fully generate the type of data that will enable us to understand and improve education, formative assessments must focus on development rather than achievement.

TOWARD AN UNDERSTANDING OF ASSESSMENT AS A DYNAMIC FORM OF PEDAGOGY

My primary interest in assessment is its potential for generating prescriptive information that can guide the development of educational and pedagogical intervention. In a very rich paper we commissioned Eleanor Armour-Thomas to write, she has presented a description of the model that she and I developed (2012) together for what we call "dynamic pedagogy." In this model, we conceptualize pedagogy as the integration of the dialectical interaction of the processes of assessment, curriculum, teaching, and learning. Dynamic pedagogy, in which assessment, teaching, and learning are inseparable, offers the best possible way of exploring and generating just the sort of prescriptive information the Gordon Commission is seeking from assessment. I use dynamic assessment to describe an approach to measurement that is as much concerned with uncovering the mental processes that examinees use in their performance as it is with the product of their performance.

Within this new model, dynamic assessment seeks to determine not only the status of examinees or learners but also the processes of learning by which that status is achieved or manifested. It is dynamic in the sense that it is adaptive to the performance of the examinee/learner and it has no fixed entry or exit points. In this way, assessment begins where the learner is, follows the learner's lead, and ends at the limit of the learner's demonstrated ability or willingness to try. Instead of standardized procedures, the assessments are tailored to the characteristics of the person being examined. Thus, the primary task is not simply to understand what the student or learner knows and can do but to elucidate the processes and conditions that the learner uses to demonstrate her/his status. In the dynamic approach, we seek to determine the conditions under which the examinee can demonstrate what she knows or the processes by which he draws from the zone of proximal development or new learning to demonstrate both intent and consolidated competence.

I feel that the dynamic assessment perspective may be more useful for providing guidance to teaching and learning than standardized assessment, which has the potential for misrepresenting the constantly changing nature of learning as the processes by which attitudes, knowledge, and skill are acquired and utilized. Additionally, I believe that the increasing concern for equity and fairness in testing requires that responsible approaches to educational assessment include attention to the quality of available teaching and learning transactions and to the sufficiency of learner's access to these experiences as part of the assessment process. If one is assessing ability to learn it may not be sufficient to simply assume that one has had or availed appropriate and sufficient opportunity to learn.

Chatterji, Koh, Everson, and Solomon (2008) describe a useful assessment technique that is designed to help students deconstruct learning tasks in any content (e.g., mathematics) area. Similar to dynamic assessment, their concept of "proximal assessment" is also embedded in the instruction, and is used as a diagnostic and instructional process during student-teacher interactions. It is continuous and useful in the planning and conduct instruction. In their research, Chatterji and her colleagues trained teachers to use proximal assessment by categorizing math problem solving (e.g., division) into specific targeted student skills. By arranging problems in order of difficulty, teachers can evaluate student learning and understanding at various steps and more precisely reveal where the student misunderstanding begins. The purpose of their assessment is to diagnose problems during the instructional process instead of at the end of the learning period. Whimbey and Lochhead have used a similar method as they debrief learners during the course of instruction seeking learner explanations for the learning tasks that they are executing. In these and other similar assessment exercises, measurement, diagnosis, prescription, teaching, and learning are integrated in the interest of student progression.

DYNAMIC PEDAGOGY

Consider the proposition that to engage in teaching one must use assessments to inquire into

- the nature and character of the learning person and his/her characteristic ways of knowing;
- what the learning person knows, needs to know, and knows how to do;
- what learning and mediating processes are associated with effective teaching and learning for this learner; and
- what is being learned by the learner and the disposition to learn it.

This is a dynamic pedagogy—a form of teaching that integrates assessment, curriculum, and instruction in the service of learning. We use the term "dynamic" to describe the process of teaching and learning in which assessment, instruction, curriculum, and learning are inseparable processes in pedagogy—and in which assessment, curriculum, and instruction constantly adapt in response to both the potential and demonstrated learner behavior. We define "pedagogy" as a form of teaching in which the actual actions taken by the teacher in these three areas are intended to promote both the process and outcomes of student learning. In order to clarify this definition of pedagogy, it is important to examine how it may be distinguished from the concept of instruction. Instruction involves the specific techniques and strategies (e.g., questioning strategies, giving feedback to students) that teachers use to engage students in classroom activities but pedagogy constitutes a broad range of elements in curriculum, assessment, and instruction that teachers orchestrate and use to promote student learning. In our definition of pedagogy, instruction is one component of an interrelated set of curricula and assessment strategies that teachers use in the service of learning.

As we have discussed in chapter 4, one of the most often cited aims of schooling in the United States is the improvement of knowledge, skills, and disposition for living in a competitive global society—an aim the educational policy apparatus has increasingly sought to achieve through standardized testing. While some forms of standardized assessment provide some information about student learning—proficiency in basic skills and domain-specific knowledge and skills—they are primarily designed for the purpose of providing comparative information about students learning at a particular point in time (e.g., end-of-year instruction) with respect to content standards. Providing credible information about how to help students learn is not their central function. If, however, assessments are to inform the improvement in learning, then they cannot function independently from the curriculum. The opportunities we give students to develop knowledge, skills, understanding, higher-order thinking, and problem solving (which indicate that learning has happened) in fact determine whether students acquire these competencies within a discipline organized around interrelated concepts and principles (the curriculum). Thus, content is an essential feature of a learning-centered assessment and its form may vary as well. For example, an assessment used to elicit information about students' prior knowledge related to solving a problem within the mathematics domain is different from an assessment used to check student's metacognitive skill while solving a problem.

Assessment is linked to learning through instruction in that the results of assessment function as feedback about strengths and weaknesses about the learner's performance in relation to a given task. In the example of problem solving, the results from assessment may be used to provide assistance in the form of instructional supports and may include modeling the problem-solving processes, reducing the difficulty level of the problem, and using hints and cues to direct the leaner to critical features of the problem to be solved. Again, the form of what we call assisted assessments may be quite varied and include open-ended questions, observations, collections of samples of student work, or their self-evaluations.

New insights about learning from research from the cognitive and learning sciences about how children learn, such as those discussed in chapter 3, should guide the next generation of assessments. However, there are other considerations. In recent years, reform-minded educational policy makers and researchers, interested in the improvement of student learning have become increasingly focused on the curriculum and how that curriculum should be taught. For example, specialized professional associations in mathematics, science, English language arts and literacy, world languages, social studies developed standards that articulate what students should know and be able to do in each discipline. Inquiry skills and conceptual understanding of core ideas in science, problem solving, communication, mathematical reasoning, and mathematical connections in mathematics, formulation of historical questions, interrogation of historical data, and employment of quantitative analysis in history are illustrative of the kinds of competencies envisioned for learners by designers of curriculum in these disciplines. How students are supported to develop these domain-specific competencies brings attention to the importance of the purpose and function of the relationship of instruction to learning. The adaptation of subject-matter knowledge for pedagogical purposes (Shulman, 1986); "psychologizing" of the subject matter (Dewey, 1902/1969); and Bruner's psychology of a subject matter (1966) are examples of instructional approaches that have their focus as the improvement of student learning. Thus, in order to understand the process and product of learning, we must understand its relationship to curriculum and instruction. However, we argue that it is the dynamic interaction of all three—assessment, curriculum, and instruction—with learning as the focus in which student learning is optimized.

Dynamic pedagogy is a sociocognitive approach to teaching in which assessment, curriculum, and instructional processes are united in the service of student learning as illustrated in figure 6.1.

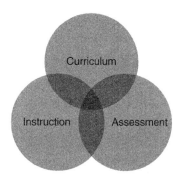

Figure 6.1   Dynamic pedagogy.

The interlocking circles indicate the interdependence of assessment, curriculum, and instruction and the jagged lines are intended to depict the dynamic interaction among these three areas of pedagogy in response to the learning strengths and needs of the learner.

The Learning Strand of Dynamic Pedagogy

Theoretical and empirical research in cognitive and learning sciences, such as those discussed in chapter 3, offer insights about the products and processes of learning, the context and conditions of their learning, and the characteristics of the learners that influence how well they learn. Within the dynamic pedagogy model, these become the focus of assessment.

Intellective Competence Is the Ultimate Outcome of Learning
The educated person in the twenty-first century needs the kinds of knowledge and skills that enable the development of intellective competence, which we have discussed in great detail in chapter 4. To be clear, I do not undervalue the importance of improving students' discipline-based knowledge and skills but see these academic achievements as instrumental to far more meaningful ends. The end goal of learning is less about what learners are expected to know and are able to do in any academic discipline of interest but more about our expectations of what they should become—autonomous, intentional learners who are sensitive,

compassionate, thinking, and productively cooperative members of human communities.

All Children Have the Potential to Learn

Several authors (Feuerstein, Rand, and Hoffman, 1979; Campione and Brown, 1987; Lidz, 1995) suggest that some children from culturally diverse backgrounds, children with learning disabilities, or students from impoverished environments have the capacity to learn more than the results of conventional tests of their abilities would indicate. "Learning potential" (Budoff, 1969), "developing expertise," and "latent abilities" (Sternberg and Grigorenko, 2000) are terms used to describe abilities that have not yet matured but can be developed through mediated learning experiences. Vygotsky (1978) used the concept of the zone of proximal development to describe the "distance between the actual developmental level as determined by independent problem solving and the level of potential development as determine through problem solving under adult guidance or in collaboration with more capable peers" (p. 86).

The Importance of Prior Knowledge for New Learning

A widely shared view about learning from a cognitive and sociocultural perspective is that new learning is shaped by prior knowledge, which is relevant to the new knowledge to be learned (Bransford and Franks, 1971; Resnick and Klopfer, 1989; Flavell, Miller, and Miller, 1993; Schneider, 1993; Anderson, 1995). Knowledge is organized in an interrelated way and stored in memory as knowledge structures. In accounting for the role of prior knowledge structures in new learning, Gagne and Dick (1983) suggest that knowledge structures help retention of new materials by providing a scaffold or framework for storage but may also modify the new information by making it "fit" the expectations of already existing knowledge structures. Although prior knowledge is necessary for new learning, researchers have found that misconceptions may impede future learning (Byrnes, 1996; DeCorte, 2003; Halpern and Hakel, 2003). Misconceptions may be described as distorted knowledge that results when new information is filtered through knowledge structures that are themselves superficial, naive, incomplete, or downright incorrect.

Building on Previous Learning to Construct New Knowledge and Skills

Once prior knowledge is activated, the learner uses that knowledge to construct new knowledge that includes both factual knowledge and conceptual understanding. Cognitive perspectives of development and learning suggest a number of factors that play a critical role in these outcomes of learning: social interaction between the learner and knowledgeable adult or capable peer (Vygotsky, 1978; Wood, Bruner, and Ross, 1976); the active role of the learner in making sense of the new information (Frederiksen and Collins, 1989); the process involved in fitting factual knowledge and conceptual understanding into existing knowledge structures (Piaget, 1970); the cultural context (Cole, Gay, Glick, and Sharp, 1971); and the structure of the knowledge to be mastered (Bruner, 1960; National Research Council, 2001a, 2001b).

Learning-Related Characteristics of the Learner

The research literature suggests that there is a variety of cognitive, emotional, and cultural patterns in an individual's response to specific environmental stimuli, persons, or events. Different terms have been used to describe these idiosyncratic responses: affective response tendency (Thomas and Chess, 1977); cognitive style (Messick, 1976); thinking style (Sternberg, 2001); learning style (Dunn and Dunn, 1978); and behavioral tendencies (Gordon, 1991). Level of energy a learner deploys, degree of focus, persistence, and intensity of effort in the learning effort are some of the behavioral manifestations of a learner's characteristics that indicate how engaged a learner is in a learning experience. These behaviors directly affect the quantity and quality of their learning. It is far more likely that a learner will be highly engaged in a task that matches her personal characteristics. Conversely, we can expect low levels of engagement from a learner whose characteristics are mismatched with the characteristics of the task at hand. One implication of this body of research is that the selection of tasks or the conditions under which tasks are made available for learners should elicit their initial interest and sustain it until successful completion of the task.

Learning Is Shaped by Social Context

As we discuss in chapter 3, theoretical and empirical studies in cognitive psychology and learning sciences hold that development, learning, and cognition are inextricably wedded to the context in which they occur (Greeno, Collins, and Resnick, 1996; Nitsche, 1997; Greeno, 1998; White and Frederiksen, 1998; Bransford, Brown, and Cocking, 1999). We define "context" as the social and physical system in which the learner participates, and we define "the learning process" as changes in participation in socially organized activity (Lave, 1988; Lave and Wenger, 1991). Several studies have demonstrated how the acquisition, understanding, and application of domain-specific concepts and principles grew out of individuals' sociocultural experiences (Saxe, 1988; Moses, Kamii, Swap, and Howard, 1989; Gutierrez, Baquedano-Lopez, and Alvarez, 1999; Ma, 1999; Valdes, 2001; Lee, 2007).

Learning Is More Than Acquiring Knowledge or
Mastering Subject Matter

After learners have acquired factual knowledge and conceptual understanding, it is important that the new learning endures over a long time and is stored well in long-term memory. To ensure permanence of new learning, learners need to consolidate the factual knowledge with deep understanding of concepts, as well as to be able to perform complex tasks automatically. Both concepts in research suggest that consolidation of learning through practice spaced over time increases retention of knowledge (Dempster, 1989; Krug, Davis, and Glover, 1990) and makes easy retrieval from memory later (Anderson, 1983). Automatic performance is also important for learning if the knowledge or skills to be learned require speed and limited mental effort. Both consolidation of learning and automatic performance of complex tasks can be achieved through practice (Bloom, 1985).

Meaningful Learning Involves the Transfer of
Learning to Other Contexts

The transfer of knowledge and understanding that has been achieved in one context to another context is evidence that meaningful new learning has occurred. Although the research is not conclusive, there appear to be some promising findings about the kinds of experiences conducive to transfer: opportunities to practice new concept or skill in different situations (Reimann and Schult, 1996; Cox, 1997); opportunities to practice retrieval of previously learned materials from long-term memory (Dempster, 1989; Glover, 1989; Dempster and Perkins, 1993); opportunities to practice varieties of applications while learning (Topping, Samuels, and Paul, 2007); opportunities to embed initial learning in a knowledge-rich context (Bransford, Brown, and Cocking, 1999); and opportunities for deep understanding of concepts and skills during initial learning of concepts and skills (Bransford and Stein, 1993).

Adept Learners Are Both Cognitively and Metacognitively Competent

Learning cannot occur without the use of some type of thinking or cognitive processes in any given task in or out of school. But the skill—and disposition—to use thinking processes effectively not only enhances learning in various academic subject areas but it also helps students achieve success in higher education and in their careers. Various scholars have developed taxonomies of thinking skills over the years. For example, Bloom and colleagues (1956) developed taxonomy of cognitive processes to describe a range from low-level processes (identifying, comparing, and labeling) to higher-level cognitive processes (analyzing, evaluating, and synthesizing) that have been used in many academic subjects and across grade levels. More recently, Beyer (1988) developed a classification of thinking processes consisting of three levels of complexity: Level I, problem solving, decision making, and conceptualizing; Level II, critical thinking skills; and Level III, information-processing skills. Like Bloom's taxonomy, these thinking processes have been infused in discipline-specific curricula in K-12 programs.

Grigorenko and Sternberg's (1997) creative, analytical, and practical thinking processes are yet another example of a cluster of thinking processes underlying successful intelligence. In a series of instructional studies, Sternberg and his colleagues found that when students were taught in a manner that best fit how they think, they outperformed students who were placed in instructional conditions that did not match their pattern of abilities (Sternberg, Torff, and Grigorenko, 1998; Sternberg, Grigorenko, Ferrari, and Clinkenbeard, 1999; Grigorenko, Jarvin, and Sternberg, 2002). These studies are important given the recent calls among educational policy makers for evidence of impact of teaching on student learning and academic achievement.

There is, of course, more to skilled thinking than the expert use of cognitive processes in learning in any given content area. Attention must also be given to the enhancement of students' awareness and use of executive thinking processes, sometimes described as metacognition (Flavell, 1979); metacomponents (Sternberg, 1985); higher-order thinking (Armour-Thomas, Bruno, and Allen, 1992). A well-established finding from cognitive science research is that competent learners are metacognitively competent (i.e., they are aware of and are able to control their own learning using a variety of self-planning, monitoring, and evaluation processes). Some researchers make a distinction between metacognitive knowledge and self-regulatory skills, although it appears that both are important for learning in a variety of domains (Palinscar and Brown, 1984; Schoenfeld, 1987; Artzt and Armour-Thomas, 1992; Hartman, 2001).

The Assessment Strand of Dynamic Pedagogy

The assessment strand of dynamic pedagogy functions within the actual implementation of a lesson and has two components. The first one is a type of "online" probe that is used

- to probe their prior knowledge, skills, and readiness for new learning;
- to check their emerging understanding of new concepts and procedures as well as misconceptions;
- to check whether they have acquired the new knowledge and skills;
- to check how well they are able to demonstrate their knowledge and skills automatically;
- to check how well they have consolidated their new learning;
- to check how well they are able to transfer it to other contexts;

- to check the mental processes engaged during learning; and
- to check disposition and motivational level while engaged in tasks.

The term has a similar meaning to Campione's (1989) "on-line diagnosis" or Slavin's (2001) "learning probes" or Gickling and Havertape's (1981) "curriculum-embedded assessments." Online probes provide iterative dynamic feedback that is used to inform adaptive instruction. Some online probes may take the form of questioning and may serve many purposes throughout the lesson. For example, questions may be used to elicit clarification on students' thinking, encourage elaboration of their ideas, or to help them make a mental bridge to another idea. Other probes may ask students to demonstrate their understanding in written form, verbally, pictorially, or through the performance of actions. Assessment in this context is formative and dynamic in nature since its results are used as feedback to inform subsequent decisions about curriculum and instruction.

The second component of assessment consists of metacognitive probes. These probes describe the variety of ways the teacher assesses the extent to which students are aware of effective learning strategies and know when and how they are to be applied. In describing this form of self-assessment, some researchers use terms such as higher-order thinking (Armour-Thomas, 1992; Frederiksen and Collins, 1989); metacognition (Flavell, 1979); regulation of cognition (Schraw, 2001); metacomponents (Sternberg, 1985); talk-aloud problem solving (Whimby and Lochhead, 1982); and self-regulated learning (Schunk and Zimmerman, 1997). Many studies have found that highly competent students are aware of and use these higher-level cognitions in their learning (Paris and Newman, 1990; Winne, 1995; Zimmerman and Risemberg, 1997; Hartman, 2001; Sternberg, 2001).

Examples of these probes include teacher questions such as the following: "What is this problem asking you to do?" "Why did you select this strategy?" "How do you know your answer is correct?" "How do you know you are on the right track?" The assessment strand is related to the curriculum strand of dynamic pedagogy in at least two ways. The first is the content of the assessment procedure itself. For example, when the assessment calls for students to show their understanding of equivalence fractions, the content of the assessment may include a word problem with information pertaining to equivalence—a topic in the grades K-4 standards-based curriculum. The second way assessment is related to curriculum is when the feedback from assessment results is used to make modifications in the teacher's subsequent curricula decisions. In the example of the assessment of equivalence, the results may show that some children may have difficulty in figuring out that two fractions are the same even though the numerators and denominators are different. The teacher may decide to use such feedback to design a task that requires students to revisit part-whole relationships, a precursor to understanding equivalent fractions. A fuller discussion of the curriculum strand follows.

The Curriculum Strand of Dynamic Pedagogy

The curriculum strand of dynamic pedagogy consists of the full range of materials (e.g., text, media, and workbooks) that embody the concepts, principles, and procedures of a discipline. Most scholars acknowledge that the term "curriculum" encompasses a body of content knowledge to be learned. But curriculum involves more than content. A more expansive notion of the concept of curriculum implies that the structure of that body of knowledge is embedded in curricula form, that is, the form in which knowledge is organized and presented within a curriculum. How that knowledge is learned (i.e., acquired, produced, or constructed) depends on what content is selected for learning and how it is communicated to the learner—decisions by the teacher that involve his/her use of instructional and assessment strategies. This notion of curriculum also implies the thinking or cognitive processes required for acquiring, producing, and ultimately transferring that body of knowledge are embedded in the curriculum. It also implies attention to characteristics or attributes of tasks that instantiate the curriculum: do tasks have attributes that arouse and sustain their motivation to learn and to use their minds well. For example, do tasks allow students to make connections to their prior knowledge and skills and to build new knowledge? Are tasks open to multiple representations and multiple ways of knowing the content? Are tasks relevant to students' personal interests and do they arouse and sustain their motivation in them until successful completion? Do tasks engage students in metacognitive and cognitive thinking about a discipline's concepts and its underlying principles? We have selected Artzt and Armour-Thomas's (2001) recommendations to teachers for designing tasks relevant for helping students to actively engage in meaningful problem solving:

1. Set tasks at the appropriate level of difficulty
2. Sequence tasks in ways that students can progress in their cumulative understanding of a particular content area
3. Select tasks with attributes that initially attract, sustain their attention, and emotional investment over time
4. Design tasks that allow students to make connections between concepts and principles earned in the past and those that they will learn in the future
5. Select appropriate modalities for representing tasks

The curriculum strand was also informed by Sternberg's theory of intelligence (1985) that posits that, along with memory, there are three kinds of abilities—analytic, creative, and practical—that draw upon a common set of components for processing information, performance, and knowledge acquisition. It is the experiences and contexts to which these components are applied that distinguish these abilities. Thus, analytical ability drawn upon information-processing components for relatively familiar tasks that require the individual to analyze, judge, evaluate, compare, and contrast while information-processing components for creative ability (e.g., ability to discover, invent, create, and explore) are applied to relatively novel tasks or familiar tasks conceptualized in a novel way. And, finally, information-processing components for practical ability (e.g., ability to put into practice, apply, use, and implement) are applied to either familiar or novel tasks in everyday contexts or settings.

We argue that if students are exposed to tasks that require them to think about concepts and procedures in these multiple ways, they are likely to learn more deeply about the content of a discipline. But even more importantly, we think that consistent and prolonged use of these kinds of cognitive and metacognitive processes for solving common and novel problems are crucial for the development of intellective competence.

The curriculum strand is related to the assessment strand in that choice of level and types of probes depend, in part, on the level and complexity of the task and its attendant cognitive and motivational demands on the learner. The example of equivalent fractions was used earlier to illustrate the relationship between the assessment strand and curriculum regarding the cognitive demands of the leaner. The example may also be used to illustrate the interdependency of curriculum and assessment when the motivation of the learner is considered. The assessment of equivalence fraction using the format of a word problem may have less motivational appeal for some children from culturally diverse background whose ways of demonstrating what they know and can do are at odds with the cultural norms of teacher-made assessment. Or, other children may have conceptual understanding of equivalence but may not be motivated to demonstrate their competence because of limitations in their proficiency with the language of assessment. Using other types of assessment to measure the same concept (e.g., asking students to show their understanding of equivalent fractions using open-ended tasks or using a different symbol system other than words to represent the problem) may yield more reliable and valid results from these types of curriculum-embedded assessments.

Another way that the curriculum strand overlaps with the assessment strand is in the design of tasks and assessments at different phases of the learning process. In helping learners to construct their own knowledge and skills related to a given domain, the teacher may design tasks different from those where the objective is to help them transfer knowledge and skills to another domain or context. To assess learning in each phase of the learning process would necessitate that the forms of assessments be compatible with the demands of the task.

The Instructional Strand of Dynamic Pedagogy

The instruction strand of dynamic pedagogy consists of a variety of strategies to help students learn and, for the most part, is based on cognitive science research. One set of strategies deal with the importance of cognitive supports to help students learn with understanding and include providing prompts, modeling, use of prompts, thinking aloud while demonstrating how to approach a task, guided practice, and supervised independent practice (Jeroen, Van Merreinboer, and Kirschner, 2007; Mayer, 2009). Another set of strategies have to do with cultivating a disposition to learn well or what some authors call "habits of mind" (Brown and Palinscar, 1989; Resnick, 2001; Costa and Kallick, 2008) or "a habit of inquiry" (Wiggins, 1993; Newman et al., 1996). Although strategies vary, depending on the scholar's perspective of what constitutes habits of mind or a habit of inquiry, they generally focus on teaching critical thinking skills (Ennis, 2001), creative problem solving (Frederiksen, 1984; Beyer, 1997), stand-alone thinking skills (Feuerstein, Rand, Hoffman, and Miller, 1980; Sternberg, Kaufman, and Grigorenko, 2008), or infusion of thinking skills in the curriculum (Perkins and Salomon, 1987; Sternberg and Spear-Swerling, 1996; Sternberg, Torff, and Grigorenko, 1998).

The instructional strand is related to the assessment strand in that results of assessment may reveal learner strengths and weaknesses that could be addressed in two ways. First, the teacher may give feedback to the learner not only in areas where he or she experienced difficulties but also feedback on how to improve one's learning. Second, based on assessment results, the teacher may use different instructional strategies when reteaching the concept or alter the pace of instruction. The example of equivalent fractions used earlier to illustrate the relationship between the assessment strand and curriculum may be used again to illustrate the overlap of assessment with instruction. For students who showed incomplete grasp of the concept of equivalent fractions, the teacher may decide to engage in a one-on-one instruction using a judicious mixture of scaffolding and guided practice strategies. In addition, the teacher may use the results from assessment to provide explicit criteria for assessing their own strengths and weakness in solving the problem of equivalent fractions. The purpose of the latter strategies is to help students develop the disposition for approaching similar problems in the future.

A FRAMEWORK FOR EXAMINING ASSESSMENT WITHIN THE DYNAMIC PEDAGOGY MODEL

Assessment decisions alone cannot inform the improvement of learning since they are inextricably wedded to other components of pedagogy, namely, curriculum and instruction. How then might assessment for learning be conceptualized given its indivisibility with curriculum and instruction? We think a multidimensional framework is necessary that conceptualizes the different types of decision making about assessments and its dynamic interdependency with curriculum and instruction and its relationship to learning. Based on our review of research on student learning, assessments, curriculum, and instruction as discussed in the previous section, we have identified four dimensions of assessment that exist at the nexus of all three components of dynamic pedagogy. Within each of the four dimensions are indicators of the specific actions and decisions that are characteristic of assessment as a dynamic component of pedagogy. The first set of actions involves establishing learning goals and objectives, and the second involves identifying the phases of learning and ensuring that assessment takes place at the critical transition points between phases.

Learning Goals and Objectives

Learning goals and objectives describe the anticipated outcomes for students at the end of a lesson, curriculum unit, or course. There at least four attributes of learning goals and objectives: specification of what is important for the learner to know and is able to do; specification of the thinking embedded in what is important for the learner to know and is able to do; the congruence of the form and content of assessment with learning goals and objectives; and accuracy and fairness of learning goals and objectives. Some questions that can be asked to assess the suitability of learning goals and objectives are as follows:

• Do learning goals and objectives indicate the domain-specific knowledge, skills, and dispositions expected of students?

- Do learning goals and objectives indicate both the cognitive and metacognitive thinking expectations for students for the expected domain-specific knowledge, skills, and disposition?
- Is the content of assessments congruent with the learning goals and objectives?
- Is the form/format of assessments congruent with the learning goals and objectives?
- Are assessments likely to yield fair and accurate results about the achievement of learning goals and objectives?

Phases of Learning

Phases of learning describe transition points in the learning cycles when learners use different thinking processes to engage the task(s) at hand. The phases are sequential in the sense that the learner has to accomplish certain tasks before proceeding to others. However, the thinking in each phase is both sequential yet recursive. For example, the thinking the learner engages in while activating prior knowledge from memory is different from the thinking he/she engages in when constructing new knowledge. Yet, the thinking processes recur when, in connecting a new concept to something familiar, the learner may have to go back into memory to verify it. We contend that learning occurs in three phases: readiness for new learning; building new learning on previous learning; and consolidating and transfer of new learning. The usefulness of assessments in each of these phases can be verified with the help of the following questions.

1. *Preparation for learning:*
   - Do assessments assess the quality of prior knowledge relevant for new learning?
   - Do assessments assess for misconceptions?
   - Do assessments assess for students' awareness and use of cognitive and metacognitive thinking process?
   - Is the form/format of assessments compatible with the function of activities in this phase of learning?
   - Is content of assessments compatible with the function of activities in this phase of learning?
   - Do assessments take into account learner characteristics?

- Do assessments take into account the context of learning?
- Do assessment results provide feedback to the learner?
- Do assessment results provide feedback to the teacher?

2. *Building on previous learning:*
   - Do assessments assess for the quality of knowledge construction and sense making?
   - Do assessments assess for the quality of emerging understanding of new concepts and procedures?
   - Do assessments assess for students' awareness and use of cognitive and metacognitive thinking process?
   - Is the form/format of assessments compatible with the function of activities in this phase of learning?
   - Is the content of assessments compatible with the function of activities in this phase of learning?
   - Do assessments take into account learner characteristics?
   - Do assessments take into account the context of learning?
   - Do assessment results provide feedback to the learner?
   - Do assessment results provide feedback to the teacher?

3. *Consolidation and transfer of new learning:*
   - Do assessments assess whether and how well learners are consolidating new learning?
   - Do assessments assess whether and how well learners are automatically engaging in new learning?
   - Do assessments assess for transfer of new learning to other contexts?
   - Is the form/format of assessments compatible with the function of activities in this phase of learning?
   - Is the content of assessments compatible with the function of activities in this phase of learning?
   - Do assessments check for students' awareness and use of lower- and higher-order thinking process?
   - Do assessments take into account learner characteristics?
   - Do assessments take into account the context of learning?
   - Do assessment results provide feedback to the learner?
   - Do assessment results provide feedback to the teacher?

In our vision of the future of assessment, the improvement of learning is its central purpose. It functions in dynamic interaction with curriculum and instruction, which themselves have the improvement of learning as its central purpose. Decisions about the form and content of assessment are informed by a sociocultural perspective of learning, curriculum, and instruction and its results are used by both the teacher and the learner to guide future teaching and learning. We put forth a multidimensional framework for organizing views of assessment as part of the teaching-learning process.

In order for this framework of assessment to truly make a difference in the lives of learners and teachers in the future, we must do the following:

1. *Make learning-centered assessments count in the evaluation of learning and teaching:* A growing trend in recent years is the use of standardized achievement test results to hold teachers, schools, and districts accountable for what students learn in a given context. Typically, tests that meet rigorous psychometric criteria of reliability and validity are used to document achievement performance of students after a year of schooling. Some educational policy makers use the results from such assessments to inform instruction in the classroom. But, as we have argued earlier, test scores do not tell the complete story on student learning and should be complemented by learning-centered assessments that are used in the classroom as a part of the learning process and therefore more closely tied to curriculum and instruction. Such assessments are oftentimes described as "formative" since its purpose is twofold: to inform the learner and the teacher about aspects of learning and teaching that are going well and aspects that need improvement. To ensure complementarity between standardized tests and learning-centered assessments, both measures would need to reflect the same subject-matter content and the same learning goals and objectives. A common form of assessment, though used for different purposes, would be a necessary requirement as well.

2. *Use computer technologies to develop learning-centered assessments:* The primary purpose of learning-centered assessments is to provide feedback to the learner and the teacher. The learner uses the feedback to improve his/her learning and the teacher uses the feedback to make modifications in his/her subsequent

curricula or instructional decisions. Management of data can be quite labor intensive and require an enormous amount of time of the classroom teacher. However, in recent years, the convergence of digitalized technologies and cognitive science have led to promising technology-based assessments that could significantly improve the efficiency of learning and teaching. For example, computer-based assessments such as the Problem Solving in Technology-Rich Environments (TRE) assess inquiry skills, provide opportunities to monitor one's efforts, and organize and report results. Moreover, the TRE approach has design features for assessing different levels of skill, representing problems in different modalities, opportunities for using different approaches to solving problems, and verifying multiple solutions. Other examples of technology-enabled assessments include simulated games in physics (e.g., Supercharged) and history (e.g., Civilization 111) that place students in roles as scientists, investigators, and doctors giving them opportunities for independent thinking and problem solving in real-life environments. Data generated from these simulations produces multiple data about students' actions and responses that may be used to guide learning and instruction. Because assessments are integrally related to curriculum and instruction, the benefits of technology-enhanced assessment would require a coordinated effort with many stakeholders among a community of stakeholders including educational policy makers, specialists in areas of curriculum, instruction, measurement, and software design.

3. *Ensure the validity and fairness of learning-centered assessments.* Learning-centered assessments must meet the validity and fairness criteria if they are to provide accurate and meaningful information for further learning and teaching. For the validity issue, this would mean using multiple measures to assess learning at any point across the learning continuum, verifying that the form and formats of assessments adequately represent the curriculum domain and that they are compatible with the process-learning goals and objectives of the lesson, unit, or course. With regard to the fairness criterion, decisions about learning-centered assessments must address the multiple diversities that learners bring

to the learning situation (e.g., differential response tendencies, limited language proficiency, and special needs).

4. *Prepare teachers.* To plan and implement assessment as a dynamic component of pedagogy would require teacher to have an understanding of how children and adolescents develop and learn from a social constructive perspective; standards-based curriculum instruction; the dynamic interdependence of curriculum, instruction, and assessment and its relationship to student learning; assessment as feedback to inform student growth in learning; and improvement in curricula and instructional decision making. But understanding of these issues is not enough. Teachers would need to have the skill to transform their understanding of the conception of assessment as a dynamic component of pedagogy into a methodology that can be implemented in the classroom. But knowing how to do so may not necessarily mean that teachers would do so since some teachers may have beliefs that are not compatible with the conception of assessment proposed in this chapter. If these ideas about assessment are to become part of teachers' daily practice, then changes would need to occur in teacher preparation programs as well as in programs for the continuing professional development of practicing teachers. Today, many teacher education programs offer coursework in child and adolescent development and learning separate from coursework in curriculum, instruction, and assessment. These learning experiences would need to be modified so that teacher candidates have an understanding of the interdependency of assessment, curriculum, and instruction and its linkage to a knowledge base on how children develop and learn. Teacher candidates would also need to be provided with opportunities for reflecting on their beliefs about assessment and learning with a view toward an acceptance that they can make a difference in children's learning and their own teaching through changes in their assessment practices.

QUALITATIVE ANALYSIS AS AN INTERIM STEP IN ACHIEVING ASSESSMENT *FOR* EDUCATION

In this chapter, we have discussed some evocative, emerging forms of assessment that, if fully realized, could truly bring about assessment *for* education. If it were to focus on informing education rather than intermittent assessment of learner status, formative assessment could be a powerful diagnostic tool for teachers; dynamic pedagogy is inherently designed to approach assessment, teaching, and learning as an interactive processes. Additionally, in chapter 5, we have observed that there are a variety of types and sources of evidence that can and should be used in assessment (beyond learner status as determined through standardized tests) and we will discuss in chapter 7 relational data management systems and tools that can enable us to analyze data from various sources in order to improve educational outcomes for all learners in a diverse student population. Still, we know that there is some length of road to travel before the way we view and use assessment is changed—from assessing what we have achieved to understanding and improving education. Until the many changes in the political and bureaucratic climate can be undertaken in order to begin maximizing the full potential of assessment, so that testing learner status for the purpose of accountability is just one of the many ways we use assessment, are we resigned to simply continuing as we have done?

We know that assessment as we currently use it has not helped us improve the overall quality of education for all learners in the United States, so continuing to use it this way seems both costly and futile. Neither can we afford to suspend assessment altogether until we have brought about a full system change in how we view assessment and gather and analyze data. So what can we do in the meantime? In 1970, as a member of the Commission on Tests convened by the College Entrance Examination Board, I prepared a brief called "Toward a Qualitative Approach to Assessment," in which I laid out a framework by which, without changing testing, we can simply make better use of the data it generates; I have excerpted this brief below. There are, of course, limitations to this approach: in it, we are still making use of data that focus on what has been developed in learners. In other words, we are still dealing with history rather than potentiality for the future. To be responsive to the commission's concern about what will really be effective in improving educational outcomes, assessment must collect and analyze data about what is currently happening in teaching and learning transactions. This is in fact one of the limitations of Else Haeussermann's (1958) otherwise tremendously powerful work: she contrived the circumstances of her research, and we at the commission ultimately wish to understand the live, real-time circumstances that facilitate engagement between teachers and students—an inquiry that is being undertaken by various anthropologists and scholars as part of a study group funded by the National Science Founded (NSF) investigating how to achieve excellence and equity in STEM (science, technology, engineering, and mathematics) achievement in a diverse learner population I am currently helming. Until we are able to begin analyzing how to enable the development of abilities rather than confirming the status of developed abilities, we may begin to analyze the data from standardized tests in such ways that allow us to begin improving educational outcomes in addition to serving the important purposes of accountability.

I began the brief with the observation that much of the impetus for developing assessment systems and mechanisms has both resulted from and been perpetuated by a supply-and-demand approach to education. This observation still holds true today. Access to a limited supply of educational opportunities has been guarded by selection procedures that prior to the twentieth century were based on the prospective student's social status. Even as opportunities have remained limited in supply, the educational enterprise has continued to place great emphasis on the selection of students and the prediction of what their performance would be when exposed to those opportunities. Binet's work on intelligence test development was directed toward the creation of an instrument that could be used to identify those pupils who were likely to benefit from schooling. Given the scarcity of educational opportunities in his time, his belief that intelligence was in fact educable did not gain favor. Society found greater utility in the promise of the predictive and selective validity of his new test. This emphasis on selection and prediction has continued even though the social conditions that gave rise to it have changed. In contemporary US society, and into the future, selection and prediction can no longer be allowed to dominate in the technology of psychoeducational appraisal. Rather, as we on the Gordon Commission concur, the stage must be shared with an emphasis on *description* and *prescription*—that is, the qualitative description of intellective function leading not to the selection of those most likely to succeed but to the prescription of the learning experiences required to more adequately insure that academic success is possible.

Psychological testing obviously can be used to measure achieved development. From those achievement patterns, subsequent achievement in the same dimensions of behavior under similar learning-experience conditions can be predicted with reasonable validity. Thus people who have learned an average amount during one learning period (high school) may be expected to learn an average amount in the next learning period (college). However, adequate attention has not been given to the facts that psychological testing can be used to describe and qualitatively analyze behavioral function to better understand the processes by which achievement is developed, to describe nonstandard achievements that may be equally functional in subsequent situations requiring adaptation, or to specify those conditions in the interaction between learner and learning experience that may be necessary to change the quality of future achievements.

Today, we remain concerned with access to higher education for larger numbers of young people and for youth from more diverse backgrounds than those from which college students were previously chosen as we were in 1970, when I wrote this brief. Now, as then, I maintain that it is not enough to simply identify the high-risk students. The tasks of assessment and appraisal in this situation are to identify atypical patterns of talent and to describe patterns of function in terms that lead to the planning of appropriate learning experiences. To conclude my brief, I made four recommendations to the College Entrance Examination Board; I believe these recommendations still resonate today:

1. The board should explore possibilities for adding to its quantitative reports on the performance of students, reports descriptive of the patterns of achievement and function derived from the

qualitative analysis of existing tests. The board's existing instruments should be examined with a view to categorization, factorial analysis, and interpretation to determine whether the data of these instruments can be reported in descriptive and qualitative ways, in addition to the traditional qualitative report.

2. It should explore the development of test items and procedures that lend themselves to descriptive and qualitative analyses of cognitive and affective adaptive functions, in addition to wider specific achievements.

3. It should explore the development of report procedures that convey the qualitative richness of these new tests and procedures to students and institutions in ways that encourage individualized prescriptive educational planning. What is called for is a statement about the nature of adaptive function in each individual that lends itself to planning a way of intervening in and facilitating his development. Patterns of strength and weakness, conditions conducive to successful coping, and conditions resulting in congruence and engagement or incongruence and alienation are examples of the kind of information required.

4. The development of research should be explored that will add to the understanding of the ways in which more traditional patterns of instruction will need to be modified to make appropriate use of wider ranges and varieties of human talent and adaptation in continuing education. It would be relatively useless to identify broader ranges of behavior if these did not have their representation in programs of instruction, and if opportunities for the use of these adaptive patterns in learning were not available to young people. Alongside modification of instruments of assessment and of procedures for appraisal there needs to be a considerable amount of attention given to modifying the curriculum and conditions under which teaching and learning occur.

Now, as then, the proposals I advanced in the brief remain very much in the conceptual stage. There is some research but little completed work that can be used to implement such a program. Yet a serious commitment to the achievement of symmetry in the continuing-education entry process, to the broadening of opportunities for access to continuing-education programs, and to the requirements of the extremely varied populations to be served demands that answers be provided to the problems implicit in these proposals.

Ultimately, if we wish to achieve the vision of assessment *for* education, we must move away from after-the-fact, decontextualized assessments and toward dynamic pedagogy, or another model like it, which integrates assessment toward informing and improving teaching and learning. In the meantime, there are interim approaches to analyzing assessment data that we might implement. But a shift toward a wider and more integrated vision of assessment is long overdue, though achievable—but only if we put our collective minds and energies behind this essential task.

BIBLIOGRAPHY

Anderson, J. R. (1983). *The architecture of cognition.* Cambridge, MA: Harvard University Press.

Anderson, J. R. (1995). *Learning and memory.* New York: Wiley.

Armour-Thomas, E., Bruno, K., & Allen, B. (1992). Toward an understanding of higher-order thinking among minority students. *Psychology in the Schools, 29,* 273–280.

Armour-Thomas, E., Chatterji M., Walker, E., Obe, V., Moore, B., & Gordon, Edmund W. (2005). *Documenting classroom processes and early effects of dynamic pedagogy: A study in selected elementary classrooms in New York.* Paper presented at the annual the of the American Educational Research Association, Montreal, Canada.

Armour-Thomas, E., & Gordon, Edmund W. (n.d.). *Toward an understanding of assessment as a dynamic component of pedagogy.* http://www.gordoncommission.org/rsc/pdf/armour_thomas_gordon_understanding_assessment.pdf

Armour-Thomas, E., & Haynes, N. (1989). Assessment of metacognition in problem solving. *Journal of Instructional Psychology, 15* (3), 87–93.

Artzt, A. F., & Armour-Thomas, E. (1992). Development of a cognitive-metacognitive framework for protocol analysis of mathematical problem solving in small groups. *Cognition and Instruction, 9,* 137–175.

Artzt, A. F., & Armour-Thomas, E. (2001). *Becoming a reflective mathematics teacher: A guide for observations and self-assessment.* Mahwah, NJ: Lawrence Erlbaum Associates.

Beyer, B. K. (1997). *Improving student thinking. A comprehensive approach.* Boston, MA: Allyn & Bacon.

Beyer, B. K. (1988). Developing a scope and sequence for thinking skills instruction. *Educational Leadership, 45* (7), 26–30.

Black, P., & Wiliam, D. (1998). Assessment and classroom learning. *Assessment in Education, 5* (1), 7–73.

Bloom, B. (1985). *Developing talent in young people.* New York: Ballantine Books.

Bloom, B. S. (Ed.). (1956). *Taxonomy of educational objectives: Handbook 1. Cognitive domain.* New York: David McKay Company, Inc.

Bransford, J. D., Brown, A. L., & Cocking, R. R. (Eds.). (1999). *How people learn: Brain, mind, experience and school.* Washington, DC: National Academy Press.

Bransford, J. D., & Franks, J. J. (1971). The abstraction of linguistic codes. *Cognitive Psychology, 2,* 331–350.

Bransford, J. D., & Stein, B. S. (1993). *The IDEAL problem solver* (2nd ed.). New York: Freeman.

Brown, A. L., & Palinscar, A. S. (1989). Guided cooperative learning and individualized knowledge acquisition. In. L. B. Resnick (Ed.), *Knowing, learning and instruction: Essays in honor of Robert Glaser* (pp. 393–451). Hillsdale, NJ: Erlbaum Associates.

Bruner, J. (1960). *The process of education.* Cambridge, MA: Harvard University Press.

Bruner, J. (1966). *Toward a theory of instruction.* Cambridge, MA: Belknap Press of Harvard University.

Budoff, M. (1969). Learning potential: A supplementary procedure for assessing the ability to reason. *Seminary. Psychiatry, 1,* 278–290.

Byrnes, J. P. (1996). *Cognitive development and learning in instructional context.* Boston, MA: Allyn & Bacon.

Calfee, R., Wilson, K. M., Flannery, B., & Kapinus, B. A. (2014). Formative assessment for the Common Core Literacy Standards. *Teachers College Record,* 116 (11), 1–32.

Campione, J. C. (1989). Assisted assessment: A taxonomy of approaches and an outline of strengths and weaknesses. *Journal of Learning Disabilities, 22* (3), 151–165.

Campione, J. C., & Brown, A. L. (1987). Linking dynamic assessment with school achievement. In C. S. Lidz (Ed.), *Dynamic assessment: An interactional approach to evaluating learning potential* (pp. 82–115). New York: Guilford Press.

Chatterji, M., Kuh, N., Everson, H., & Solomon, P. (2008). *Mapping cognitive pathways in mastering long division: A case study of grade 5–6 learners supported with a dynamic model of proximal assessment and learner diagnosis.* Paper presented at the annual meeting of the American Educational Research Association, New York.

Cole, M., Gay, J., Glick, J., & Sharp, D. W. (1971). *The cultural context of learning and thinking.* New York: Basic Books.

Costa, A. L., & Kallick, B. (2008). *Learning and leading with habits of mind.* Alexandria, VA: Association for Supervision and Curriculum.

Cox, B. D. (1997). The rediscovery of the active learner in adaptive contexts: A developmental-historical analysis of transfer of training. *Educational Psychologist, 32,* 41–55.

DeCorte, E. (2003). Transfer as the productive use of acquired knowledge, skills, and motivations. *Current Directions in Psychological Science, 12* (4), 142–146.

Dempster, F. N. (1989). Spacing effects and their implications for theory and practice. *Education Psychology Review, 1,* 309–330.

Dempster, F. N., & Perkins, P. G. (1993). Revitalizing classroom assessment: Using tests to promote learning. *Journal of Instructional Psychology, 20,* 197–203.

Dewey, J. (1902/1969). *The child and the curriculum.* Chicago: Chicago University Press.

Dixon-Román, E. J. (2011). Assessment to inform teaching and learning. *Assessment, Teaching, & Learning, 1,* (2), 1–8.

Dunn, R., & Dunn, K. (1978). *Teaching students through their individual learning styles.* Reston, VA: Reston.

Ennis, R. (1985). Goals for a critical thinking curriculum. *Developing minds: A resource book for teaching thinking.* Alexandria, VA: Association for Supervision and Curriculum Development.

Feuerstein, R., Rand, Y., & Hoffman, M. B. (1979). *The dynamic assessment of retarded performers: The learning potential assessment devise theory. Instruments and techniques.* Baltimore, MD: University Park Press.

Feuerstein, R., Rand, Y., Hoffman, M. B., & Miller, R. (1980). *Instrumental enrichment.* Baltimore: University Park Press.

Flavell, J. H. (1979). Metacognition and cognitive monitoring: A new era of cognitive developmental inquiry. *American Psychologist, 34,* 906–911.

Flavell, J. R., Miller, P. H., & Miller, S. A. (1993). *Cognitive development* (3rd ed.). Upper Saddle Road, NJ: Prentice Hall.

Frederiksen, J. R., & Collins, A. (1989). A systems approach to educational testing. *Educational Researcher, 18,* 27–32.

Frederikson, N. (1984). Implications of cognitive theory for instruction in problem solving. *Review of Educational Research, 54,* 3, 363–407.

Gagne, R. M., & Dick, W. (1983). Instructional psychology. *Annual Review of Psychology, 34* (1), 261–295.

Gickling, E., & Havertape, J. (1981). *Curriculum-based assessment (CBA).* Minneapolis, MN: National School Psychology In-service Training Network.

Glaser, R., Chudowsky, N., & Pellegrino, J. W. (Eds.). (2001). *Knowing What Students Know: The Science and Design of Educational Assessment.* Washington, DC: National Academies Press.

Glover, J. A. (1989). The "testing" phenomenon: Not gone but nearly forgotten. *Journal of Educational Psychology, 81,* 392–399.

Gordon, Edmund W. (1970). *Toward a qualitative approach to assessment. Report of the Commission on Tests, II. Briefs* (pp. 42–46). New York: College Entrance Examination Board.

Gordon, Edmund. W. (1991). Human diversity and pluralism. *Educational Psychologist, 26,* 99–108.

Gordon, Edmund. W. (1998). *Toward a definition of pedagogy.* Working paper prepared for the National Research Council's Committee on Early Childhood Pedagogy.

Gordon, Edmund. W. (2001). *Affirmative development of academic abilities.* Pedagogical Inquiry and Praxis, No. 2., Institute for Urban and Minority Education, Teachers College, Columbia University.

Gordon, Edmund. W. (2002). Personal communication.

Gordon, Edmund. W., & Armour-Thomas, E. (2006). *The effects of dynamic pedagogy on the mathematics achievement of ethnic minority students* (RM06224). Storrs, CT: The National Research Center on the gifted and talented, University of Connecticut.

Greeno, J. G. (1998). The situativity of knowing, learning, and research. *American Psychologist, 53* (1), 5–26.

Greeno, J. G., Collins, A. M., & Resnick, L. R. (1996). Cognition and learning. In D. C. Berliner & R. C. Calfe (Eds.), *Handbook of educational psychology* (pp. 14–46). New York: Macmillan.

Grigorenko, E. L., Jarvin, L. & Sternberg, R. J. (2002). School-based tests of the triarchic theory of intelligence: Three settings, three samples, three syllabi. *Contemporary Educational Psychology, 27,* 167–208.

Grigorenko, E. L., & Sternberg, R. J. (1997). Styles of thinking, abilities, and academic performance. *Exceptional children, 63* (3), 295–312.

Gutierrez, K., Baquedano-Lopez, P., & Alvarez, H. (1999). A cultural-historical approach to collaboration: Building a culture of collaboration through hybrid language practices. *Theory into Practice, 38* (2), 87–93.

Haertel, E. (2014). Reflections on the Gordon Commission. *Teachers College Record, 116* (11), 1–6.

Haeusserman, E. (1958). *Developmental potential of preschool children: An evaluation of intellectual, sensory, and emotional functioning.* New York: Grune & Stratton.

Halpern, D. F., & Hakel, M. D. (2003). Applying the science of learning to the university and beyond: Teaching for long-term retention and transfer. *Change, 35* (4), 37–41.

Hartman, H. J. (2001). Developing students' metacognitive knowledge and skill. Metacognitive. In H. J. Hartman (Ed.), *Metacognition in learning and instruction: Theory, research and practice* (pp. 33–68). Boston, MA: Kluwer Academic Publishers.

Jeroen, J., van Merrienboer, G., & Kirschner, P. A. (2007). *Ten steps to complex learning*. Mahwah, NJ: Lawrence Erlbaum Associates.

Krug, D., Davis, T. B., & Glover, J. A. (1990). Massed versus distributed reading: A case of forgetting helping recall? *Journal of Educational Psychology, 82*, 366–371.

Lave, J. (1988). *Cognition in practice: Mind, mathematics and culture in everyday life*. Cambridge, UK: Cambridge University Press.

Lave, J., & Wenger, E. (1991). *Situated learning: Legitimate peripheral participation*. Cambridge, UK: Cambridge University Press.

Lee, C. A. (2007). *Culture, literacy and learning: Taking bloom in the midst of the whirlwind*. New York: Teachers College Press.

Lidz, C. S. (1995). Dynamic assessment and the legacy of L. S. Vygotsky. *School Psychology International, 16*, 143–153.

Ma, L. (1999). *Knowing and teaching elementary mathematics*. Mahwah, NJ: Lawrence Erlbaum.

Mathematics Learning Study Committee. (2001). *Adding It Up: Helping Children Learn Mathematics*. Washington, DC: National Academies Press.

Mayer, R. (2009). Constructivism as a theory of learning versus constructivism as a prescription for instruction. In S. Tobias & T. M. Duffy (Eds.), *Constructivist instruction: Success or failure?* (pp. 184–200). New York: Taylor & Francis.

McManus, S. (2008). *Attributes of effective formative assessment*. Washington, DC: Council of Chief State School Officers.

Messick, S. (1976). Personalities consistencies in cognition and creativity. In S. Messick (Ed.), *Individuality in learning* (pp. 4–22). San Francisco: Jossey-Bass.

Moses, R. P., Kamii, M., Swap, S. M., & Howard, J. (1989). The algebra project: Organizing in the spirit of Ella. *Harvard Educational Review, 59* (4), 423–443.

Newman, F. M., et al. (1996). *Authentic achievement: Restructuring schools for intellectual quality*. San Francisco: Jossey-Bass.

Nitsche, K. E. (1997). *Structuring decontextualized forms of knowledge*. Unpublished doctoral dissertation, Vanderbilt University.

Palinscar, A. S., & Brown, A. L. (1984). Reciprocal teaching of comprehension-fostering and comprehension-monitoring activities. *Cognition and Instruction, 1* (2), 117–175.

Paris, S. G., & Newman, R. S. (1990). Developmental aspects of self-regulated learning. *Educational Psychologist, 25*, 87–102.

Pellegrino, J. W., Chudowsky, N., & Glaser, R. (2001). *Knowing what students know: The science and design of educational assessment*. Washington, DC: National Academy Press.

Perkins, D. N., & Salomon, G. (1987). Transfer and teaching thinking. In D. N. Perkins, J. Lochhead, & J. Bishop (Eds.), *The second international conference* (pp. 285–303). Hillsdale, NJ: Lawrence Erlbaum Associates.

Piaget, J. (1970). Piaget's theory. In. P. H. Mussen (Ed.), *Carmichael's manual of psychology* (pp. 11–23). New York: Wiley.

Reimann, P., & Schult, T. J. (1996). Turning examples into cases: Acquiring knowledge structures for analogical problem solving. *Educational Psychologist, 31* (2), 123–132.

Resnick, L. B. (2001). Making America smarter: The real goal of school reform. *Developing minds: A resource book for teaching thinking, 3,* 3–6.

Resnick, L. B., & Klopfer, L. E. (1989). Toward the thinking curriculum: An overview. In L. B. Resnick & L. E. Klopfer (Eds.), *Toward the curriculum: Current cognitive research* (pp. 1–18). Alexandria, VA: Association for Supervision and Curriculum Development.

Saxe, G. B. (1988). Candy selling and math learning. *Educational Researcher, 17* (6), 14–21.

Schneider, W. (1993). Domain-specific knowledge and memory performance in children. *Educational Psychology Review, 5,* 257–273.

Schoenfeld, A. H. (1987). What's all the fuss about metacognition? In A. H. Schoenfeld (Ed.), *Cognitive science and mathematics education* (pp. 189–215). Hillsdale, NJ: Lawrence Erlbaum Associates.

Schraw, G. (2001). Promoting general metacognitive awareness. In H. J. Hartman (Ed.), *Metacognition in learning and instruction: Theory, research and practice* (pp. 3–16). London: Kluwer.

Schunk, D. H., & Zimmerman, B. J. (1997). Social origins of self-regulatory competence. *Educational Psychologist, 32,* 195–208.

Shulman, L. S. (1986). Those who understand: Knowledge growth in teaching. *Educational Researcher, 15,* 4–14.

Slavin, R. E. (2001). *Educational psychology: Theory and practice.* New York: Allyn & Bacon.

Sternberg, R. J. (1977). *Intelligence, information processing, and analogical reasoning: The componential analysis of human abilities.* Hillsdale, NJ: Erlbaum.

Sternberg, R. J. (1985). *Beyond IQ: A triarchic theory of human intelligence.* Cambridge, MA: Cambridge University Press.

Sternberg, R. J. (2001). Metacognition, abilities and developing expertise. In H. J. Hartman (Ed.), *Metacognition in learning and instruction: Theory, research and practice* (pp. 247–260). Boston, MA: Kluwer Academic Publishers.

Sternberg, R. J., & Grigorenko, E. L. (2000). *Dynamic testing: The nature and measurement of learning potential.* MA: Cambridge University Press.

Sternberg, R. J., Grigorenko, E. L., Ferrari, M., & Clinkenbeard, P. (1999). A triarchic analysis of an aptitude-treatment interaction. *European Journal of Psychological Assessment, 15* (1), 1–11.

Sternberg, R. J., Kaufman, J., & Grigorenko, E. L. (2008). *Applied intelligence.* New York: Cambridge University Press.

Sternberg, R. J., & Spear-Swerling, L. (1996). *Teaching for thinking.* Washington, DC: American Psychological Association.

146   THE TESTING AND LEARNING REVOLUTION

Sternberg, R. J., Torff, B., & Grigorenko, E. L. (1998). Teaching for
successful intelligence raises school achievement. *Phi Delta Kappan*,
79, 667–669.

Thomas, A., & Chess, S. (1977). *Temperament and development.* New
York: Brunner/Mazel.

Topping, K., Samuels, J., & Paul, T. (2007). Does practice make perfect? Independent reading quantity, quality, and student achievement.
Learning and Instruction, 17 (3), 253–264.

Valdes, G. (2001). *Learning and not learning English: Latino students in
American schools.* New York: Teachers College Press.

Vygotsky, L. S. (1978). *Mind in society.* M. Cole V. John-Steiner, S.
Scribner, & E. Souberman (Eds.), Cambridge, MA: Harvard University
Press.

Walker, E. N., Armour-Thomas, E., & Gordon, Edmund W. Gordon
(2007). *Dynamic pedagogy in diverse elementary classrooms: A comparison of two teachers' instructional strategies.* National Council of
Teachers ofMathematics (NCTM) Mathematics for All Book Series.

Whimby, A., & Lochhead, J. (1982). *Problem solving and comprehension.*
Hillsdale, NJ: Lawrence Erlbaum Associates.

White, B. Y., & Frederiksen, J. R. (1998). Inquiry, modeling and metacognition: Making science accessible to all students. *Cognition and
Instruction, 16* (1), 3–118.

Wiggins, G. (1993). Assessment: Authenticity, context and validity. *Phi
Delta Kappan, 74*, 200–214.

Wilson, S. M., Shulman, L. S., & Richert, A. (1987). 150 different ways of
knowing: Representations of knowledge in teaching. In J. Calderhead
(Ed.), *Exploring teachers' thinking* (pp. 104–124). Sussex, UK: Holt,
Rinehart & Winston.

Winne, P. H. (1995). Inherent details in self-regulated learning.
Educational Psychologist, 30, 173–187.

Wood, D., Bruner, J. S., & Ross, G. (1976). The role of tutoring in problem solving. *Journal of Child Psychology and Psychiatry, 17*, 89–100.

Zimmerman, B. J., & Risemberg, R. (1997). Self-regulatory dimensions
of academic learning and motivation. In G. D. Phye (Ed.), *Handbook of
academic learning: Construction knowledge* (pp. 105–125). San Diego,
CA: Academic Press.

7

New Data Collection and Analysis Methods Offer Powerful Insights into Performance

At a recent visit to my general practice doctor, I noticed a curious change in the way he related to my health and me. During the course of our entire half-hour-long interaction, he seemed to be far more intently focused on the laptop in front of him than on me, and when I commented on this, he told me that the best care he could give me was by looking at the many data collected from my various doctors and my past visits instead of by making physical contact with me. I realized that the gold standard of patient care in modern medicine today is to understand the relationship between various data points in a patient's history. Where he once had to use a stethoscope or otoscope to gather evidence for his analysis, my doctor could now look to historic data for evidence on how I may or may not be progressing or functioning. Health care today is less about "care" and more about how the doctor can use analysis to inform and improve the patient's "health."

Although the medical establishment has not yet achieved the complete digitalization of records it has been pushing for, it is still beginning to gain purchase in a number of research universities, private practice, and government programs. Certainly, medical practice and health care in the United States can certainly be improved but some aspects of its praxis (although not its delivery) is the best in the world, and modern medical praxis is heavily grounded in the use of electronic digital information management in which relational analysis management and interpretation is key. Just as measurement science may be excessively focused on the measurement of status to the neglect of processes in dynamic interaction, the management and use of education measurement data has also been insensitive to the process relations contained in these data. The Gordon Commission's work implies that the relational analysis of education data is necessary to the understanding of teaching and learning and essential to its informed practice and improvement.

The model I carry in my head is the classroom teacher who sits there with her computer. She has an interest in monitoring or assessing whether learning is occurring at several levels. Whether she is monitoring under what conditions or with what characteristics individual students, groups of students, or the whole class is learning, she is examining the relationship between different points of data. Relational data analysis is an approach that will enable her to answer these questions; or, if she is already attempting to analyze data relationally, new tools in relational data analytics will enhance the answers to these questions. In this chapter, we will discuss the concept of relational data analysis, the need for and emergence of relational data management systems in contemporary educational praxis, some of the barriers to its full adoption, and its implications for enabling assessment *for* education.

THE PROMISE AND POTENTIAL OF RELATIONAL DATA ANALYSIS

Historically, significant advances in scientific understanding have followed advances in measurement and observation. As the *resolving* power of an instrument increased, so have gains in the understanding of the phenomena being observed. An example is the microscope, which led to insights, verification, and new research questions and theories in the three hundred years since its invention. The microscope's resolution—the degree of detail that could be distinguished in an image—allowed observation of processes and states that were previously unobservable.

We are now approaching a similar potential in the measurement of students' learning processes using technology-based tasks. Technology-based tasks can be instrumented to record fine-grained observations about what students do in the task as well as capture the context surrounding the behavior. Advances in how such data are conceptualized, in storing and accessing large amounts of data— what we have referred to in chapters 3 and 5 as "big data" or the "Digital Ocean"—and in the availability of analysis techniques that provide the capability to discover patterns from big data are spurring innovative uses for assessment and instructional purposes. One significant implication of the higher resolving power of technology-based measurement is its use to improve learning via individualized instruction by bringing into view previously unseen components.

As we discussed in chapter 3, among the many changing paradigms that are shaping the field of pedagogy *is* emerging technologies, which promise not only opportunities for personalized or individualized learning but also offer many new ways of capturing and analyzing data. The term "relational database" was invented by E. F. Codd at IBM in 1970; gradually, it came to describe a broader class of database systems that present data in relation to each other. Data have relationships with each other but until the era of big data and digitalization—which have drastically changed the quantity, availability, and storability of data—these relationships were often difficult to discern. In a relational database system, it is now possible for an analyst to query multiple databases to glean information about individuals, collections of individuals, and collections of groups and to analyze information trends over time.

If purpose of assessment is to inform and improve, then the data must be analyzed and presented in a manner that reveals its meaning for effective teaching and learning. That means revealing of relationships between specific assessment data points and data referable to learner characteristics and behaviors, conditions of learning, instructional programs, and contexts. This list is not exhaustive of all the relationships we can and should analyze through relational data systems in order to understand and improve the processes of teaching and learning but it illustrates some of the potentialities for a deeper analysis of assessment and student data that currently eludes us.

In a paper he prepared for the Gordon Commission and later finalized for publication in a special issue of *Teachers College Record* (2014), Greg K. W. K. Chung, senior researcher at the National

Center for Research on Evaluation, Standards, and Student Testing (CRESST) in UCLA's Graduate School of Education and Information Studies, writes that there is little doubt that as the number of learning applications on digital platforms increases—from transmedia learning apps and games to online assessment—the generation of huge quantities of learning-related data will also increase. If education follows industries that target individuals such as retailing, manufacturing, and health care, there will be a widespread interest in how these data could be used to improve student learning and teaching (DOE, 2010; Bienkowski, Feng, and Toyama, 2011; Manyika et al., 2011; Bienkowski, Feng, and Means, 2012). A key issue is how to leverage these data to measure what students understand and can do to derive meaningful measures of cognitive and affective processes and to develop capabilities for precise diagnosis and targeting of instruction.

THE NEED FOR DATA COLLECTION AND EVALUATION

The problem in identifying specific factors and patterns that influence achievement may be related to the fact that the interventions of the variables grounded in these several perspectives affect not only the impact of each but also the way the variables interact with each other from one situation to the other. It is thus important that those responsible for teaching and learning activities not only understand these dynamic interactions but also use that understanding to inform decisions regarding policy and practice to improve pedagogy and learning.

Particular kinds of decision making must be informed by relevant information on students, staff, program, and the deployment of resources. Fortunately, new computer technology increases educators' capacities to use data systematically to manipulate the interactions inherent in teaching and learning situations. Data systems currently exist in most education institutions, especially in public education systems, but the knowledge to use data to improve teaching and learning on macro levels (i.e., district, program, and school) and on micro levels (including classrooms and individual learner situations) is lacking. Thus, we need to identify the variables that influence teaching and learning, and develop efficient measurement and data gathering systems that incorporate them. In addition, we need to invest in capacity building—training administrators, supervisors, and teachers—so that personnel can use the data to inform daily decisions.

LEVELS OF DATA USEFUL FOR UNDERSTANDING STUDENT PERFORMANCE

Chung (2012) writes that for understanding a student's knowledge and skills, it is helpful to view data at three levels. Each level of data represents different level of aggregation and can be used to answer different kinds of questions. At the highest level of aggregation is system-level data. For example, the data housed in a student information system (SIS) reflect the indicators important to an institution. In a university, these data would include students' course-taking information, course grades, high school information, and demographic information. These kinds of data allow institutions to ask questions about system-level issues such as student retention rates, graduation rates, and time to degree. Educational measurement often generates individual-level data. Some examples include total score on an achievement test, scores on a performance task, or scores on individual items in a test. In general, this level has been the finest-grain size used in educational measurement. More recently, there has been interest in the use of data at an even finer level of detail and made practical only in technology-based applications (e.g., Romero, Ventura, Pechenizkiy, and Baker, 2011). Transaction-level data reflect a student's interaction with a system where the interaction may be an end in itself (e.g., the action a learner performs as part of gameplay) or a means to an end (e.g., the act of uploading an assignment in a learning management system). In either case, these interactions are increasingly becoming data sources about students' moment-to-moment choices on some task and are beginning to be captured and stored in a format suitable for analyses of student learning.

ELEMENTS OF DATA GATHERING SYSTEM

According to CRESST, there are three building blocks of accountability (in addition to several key capacities) that support the development and implementation of a comprehensive and effective accountability and data management system: (1) a set of policies and procedures that encourages and supports effective teaching and learning; (2) differential strategies for regularly eliciting and managing information that not only indicate how schools are functioning for all students but also identify specific areas of the school context that may influence the school's success of failure; and (3) mechanisms for reconsidering school practices when students are not well served.

Information appropriately managed through technology enables the tailoring of data analysis and management in ways implicit in pedagogical approaches, which were first proposed as early as the mid-twentieth century. Tyler (1949) advocated the use of data from tests and other assessments for data-based decision making in the classroom for instructional purposes. Flanagan (1969) suggested that one of the ways to address the special and individual needs of students and of specific groups of learners is to customize the pedagogy. Moreover, Flanagan (1969) and Glaser (1967), independently working on related models, asserted that individualized and customized teaching and learning would rest on teacher's capacity to manage large amounts of student and instructional data and materials as the basis for decisions concerning the design and management of teaching and learning transactions. These ideas were never fully implemented, partially because educators did not have the capacity to manage the information necessary to design, deliver, and evaluate individualized instruction.

The capacity to analyze program, staff, and student data to better inform education decisions now exists. In the United States, we have the technology to document the dynamic interactions between multiple variables in diverse teaching and learning situations. We can quickly examine relationships among a wide range of dependent and independent variables to determine the interaction of demographic characteristics, learning behaviors, class size, instructional behavior, teacher characteristics, curriculum demands, time on task, attendance patterns, resource availability, and resource utilization, for example. Through the use of relational program and student data management systems, it is possible to identify program, staff, and student variables that are associated with particular pedagogical outcomes.

There are many decisions being made at any given time in an education ecosystem, and it is not only teachers who need to make informed decisions. Administrators and policy makers also need to make decisions that require their understanding of education data and information on the functioning of the various personnel, students, programs, and systems for which they are responsible. Yet only a few school districts have the capacity to manage these data efficiently and in ways that can inform critical decisions and, equally important, anticipate other intended and unintended consequences. Existing databases in school, district, and state systems are generally uncoordinated, redundant, and/or have large gaps in essential information. Current systems of data management are built in response to top-down, politically driven, often legislative actions, with little cognizance of the relational information needs of the people who make day-to-day education policy and practice decisions. Guidance counselors, instructional supervisors, and teachers who could use these data are often overwhelmed by the tasks of searching out the relevant information to meet their decision-making needs.

Broadly speaking, the information products of these data management systems are limited only by the character and quality of a school system's data inputs and the particular questions asked of the system. Given the imperative to uncouple achievement from social divisions, such as class, ethnicity, gender, first language, and, more recently, the goals of NCLB legislation, one of the critically important advantages of a data management system is its capacity to disaggregate data by specified input and outcome variables and to identify relationships between them. In addition, Lezotte and Jacoby (1992) suggest that a primary purpose of these analytic processes is to provide individual schools and districts with the mechanism for gauging their own effectiveness.

To that end, specific procedures can be used to identify the different subsets of students who master (or fail to master) the curriculum, by school, grade level, program, and/or course. An analysis of achievement by grade level, for example, can enable principals and district supervisors to monitor whether students of differing socioeconomic levels, races, and gender are mastering the essential student outcomes and whether the curriculum is equitably available, taught to, and mastered by all students, especially those from disadvantaged and underrepresented groups. The disaggregation of data that the federal government proposes to use in monitoring and monetarily rewarding or punishing states whose schools do not demonstrate improvements on standardized tests (James, Jurich, and Estes, 2001) is also a practical, hands-on process that enables a school to answer two critical questions: For whom is its curriculum effective? And what does the curriculum teach?

EXAMPLES OF DATA MANAGEMENT SYSTEMS

Mary Ann Lachat played a pivotal role in initiating one of the most comprehensive relational data management systems we have reviewed. The SOCRATES™ system (developed by Lachat and the Center for Resource Management [CRM]) was designed to enable the management and disaggregation of data, to track the programs and practices to which students have been exposed, and to keep a cumulative record of the knowledge and skills students may or may not have acquired. According to CRM, the SOCRATES™ system has import and data merge capabilities that can be used to integrate data from school records, administrative files, and standardized assessments to answer a wide range of questions.

Obviously, other programs exist and are being developed. For example, I was involved in the conceptualization of programs developed several years ago for the Prince Georges County Maryland Public Schools by the College Board's Equity 2000 initiative and the Montgomery County Maryland Public Schools. Their goal was to encourage teachers and principals to collect and interpret student, staff, and program data by providing access to desktop computers programmed to process such data. While the technical demands were modest, the program enabled immediate access to both aggregated and disaggregated student and program data.

Personnel were thus able to monitor the dynamics of student placements, evaluate program effectiveness, gauge individual and collective student progress, and examine the relationships between these variables. The difficulties in these efforts were related to (1) gaining access to the relevant data to enter into the systems, (2) designing and managing the data entry process, and (3) developing the human capital necessary to support and utilize the systems.

An interesting effort to apply data-driven decision making was evaluated by Madhabi Chatterji of Teachers College, Columbia University. It involved using district-level databases in a deeds assessment for the Safe and Drug Free Schools (SDFS) program in two Florida school districts for initiating new programs. The effort was made in response to a state-sponsored competition for federal funds under the Goals 2000 initiative at a midsize Florida school district. A review of the literature on student risk and resiliency factors by the School and Community Advisory Council enabled the identification of three categories of indicators that would define a "high needs school" for the SDFS program. Three categories of data elements, extracted from the district's management information system and the Florida Information and Resource Network System, included (1) academic risk indicators (student achievement data), (2) demographic risk indicators (socioeconomic status, mobility, and attendance): and (3) social-behavioral risk indicators (crime, violence, truancy, and substance abuse). Reports showing school-level aggregates of individual data elements and their interrelationships were prepared for district-level decision makers. Subsequently, stakeholders were led by the evaluator through a systematic set of steps to arrive at a ranked list of schools that had the highest needs profiles for SDFS funding.

While space constraints prevent an elaboration of all existing relational data management programs, the following programs/data support resources might be of interest:

- The Quality School Portfolio (QSP; developed by CRESST) is a web-based mechanism for disaggregating tests and other data and examining data as mandated by state accountability systems and by the NCLB legislation.

- EDexplore™, developed by Edsmart Inc., manages data processes from data extraction and transformation to loading and hosting the resulting database on its servers. Clients, who gain access via the Internet, receive training and ongoing support on the use of data to inform decisions;
- ACCOUNT allows selected personnel access to relevant information concerning related and disparate aspects of schooling, including trends in attendance, test scores, finances, and student demographics. Similar to EDexplore™, ACCOUNT also integrates separate databases into a data warehouse.

Additional data disaggregation and management tools have been identified by Slowinski (2002; described in the box on p. 3). While these resources are clearly useful, it is important to address the criteria to which relational data management systems should adhere. CRESST suggests that data management systems should not only utilize various types of data from diverse sources but should also include relevant information concerning program, student, and staff characteristics to (1) provide contexts for interpreting student achievement; (2) account for student outcomes such as achievement, attendance, mobility, and rates of retention in grade, dropout, and graduation; and (3) provide data not only on the available instructional resources and curriculum materials but also on the degree to which students are provided with adequate opportunities to master content specified instate and other curriculum standards.

Chung (2012) identifies two examples of how data can be used to individualize teaching and learning. The first example is the use of learning analytics in a higher education setting that fuses macro-level data from the institution's SIS with usage data from the institution's learning management system (LMS) to predict individual student success in a course. The second set of examples focuses on the derivation of fine-grained measures to understand student learning processes.

Learning analytics is the "use of analytic techniques to help target instructional, curricular, and support resources to support the achievement of specific learning goals" (van Barneveld, Arnold, and Campbell, 2012, p. 8). The goal of learning analytics is to enable instructors and institutions to tailor the educational experiences of individual students in near real-time. Example applications include predicting student outcomes, creating course dashboards, evaluating curriculum, and identifying students at risk of failing (Bach, 2010). Learning analytics is expected to be implemented in an increasing number of institutions over the next five years (Johnson, Adams, and Cummins, 2012). One example of learning analytics is the Signals project at Purdue University (Campbell and Oblinger, 2007). Signals began as an initiative to predict student success (i.e., grades) in a course. Signals assumed student success was a function of the student's background (e.g., aptitude, prior experiences) and the student's effort in a course. One important function of the Signals system is to allow an instructor to predict individual student risk. From the perspective of relational data management, the designers of Signals asked a key question: Could the information from existing data stores designed for one purpose be used to make point predictions about an individual for the more nuanced purpose of identifying individuals at risk of not being successful? Signals exemplifies a practical approach to relational data management to support student learning.

One limitation of general-purpose systems designed to support student learning (e.g., an LMS) is that they are designed to host content and not designed to measure learners' interaction with that content. The quality of the measures derived from a general-purpose system may be limited to behavior such as frequency of access, time spent on a task, textual data that are entered by students in a discussion board, and student ratings. Usage as a proxy for learning outcomes is less desirable than measures derived from students' direct interaction with a task, which has two dimensions: outcome measures, which address whether students were able to complete the task, and process measures, which address what students were doing throughout the task. In the first dimension, performance on the task itself is taken as an index of understanding. This has been the traditional approach of online performance assessments (Baker, Chung, and Delacruz, 2008). The second approach is to derive meaningful measures from students' interaction with the system as they attempt to accomplish the objectives of the task. The more the process measures target students' behavior directly relevant to achieving the outcome, the higher the measures' diagnostic value and their potential to predict the outcome.

Chung (2012) then goes on to offer three illustrative examples drawn from research conducted at the CRESST. The examples are illustrative and not intended to be a comprehensive review of the literature. A line of research asked three questions related to online measurement of learning processes: (1) To what extent does students' online behavior relate to their cognitive processing? (2) To what extent can students' online behavior be used to model their problem-solving process? (3) To what extent can students' online behavior be used diagnostically to reveal understandings and misconceptions? The first question was addressed by examining the extent to which measures based on students' online behavior correlated with measures based on their cognitive processes (as measured via their think-alouds). The second question examined user-interface design to extract meaningful data from students' interaction with a simulator. The interface ensured that the measurement reflected a user's intent, which is critical when attempting to model students' problem-solving processes. The last question addressed both ideas in a single application: games for learning. In this case, the extraction of meaningful data is baked into the task itself. Well-designed games are inherently engaging and gameplay behavior is purposeful. When success in the game requires specific domain knowledge and the "game mechanics" require use of that domain knowledge, then the gameplay behavior itself reflects students' understanding. Underlying all three questions is the collection of fine-grained behavioral data and its use to gain insight about students' learning processes.

IMPLICATIONS

Chung (2012) notes that the idea of increased resolving power based on fine-grained data was presented in the context of relational management of educational data. At one end of the data spectrum was the example of Signals, which was used as an example of fusing SIS and LMS data to predict individual student success in a course. At the other end of the data spectrum was the set of examples on the use of fine-grained data on online behavior to infer student learning processes and understanding.

An implication of the availability of such data, writes Chung, is the development of adaptive educational systems. General models of adaptation have been established in the literature and are referred to as macroadaptation or microadaptation (e.g., Glaser, 1977; Corno and Snow, 1986; Park and Lee, 2003). Recent work on adaptivity with computer-based technology has focused on the questions of what to adapt and how to adapt (e.g., Shute and Zapata-Rivera, 2012). Macroadaptation refers to the adaptation of the instructional environment to the individual such as a teaching strategy, a prescribed curriculum plan based on students' needs (e.g., an Individualized Education Program, or IEP), and allocation of instructional resources and materials to accommodate individual student needs. In micro-adaptation, the instructional decisions are based on moment-to-moment interactions with a student such as in a one-on-one tutoring situation or in computer-based situations that monitor and respond to a student's ongoing progress on a task. In either adaptation model, the goal is to adapt instruction as precisely as possible to the particular student's need with the goal of maximizing learning outcomes. He then describes the role relational educational data has in each of these approaches. In the following sections offering an overview of adaptive systems to support teaching and personalizations, we have excerpted and paraphrased from Chung (2014).

Adaptive Systems to Support Teaching

With respect to supporting teaching, the development and use of data-driven systems designed specifically to support educational improvement in K-12 settings was pioneered by Baker (2000) with the QSP system. QSP provided the capability for administrators and teachers to easily import student data at the individual level, including background and demographic information, standardized test scores, benchmark test scores, and whatever other data were available. Graphing, analyses, and a variety of reporting formats were part of the standard QSP services. Unlike Signals, QSP was designed to provide more analytical control that would allow administrators and teachers to identify areas in need of improvement specific to the user's district, school, or classroom.

The reporting of diagnostic information about the particular concepts and misconceptions to the teacher and student may be the area of greatest leverage when using relational management systems. As discussed in the examples, transaction-level data appear to reflect students' underlying cognitive processes and knowledge. When computer-based applications (e.g., games) are designed around learning objectives and purposively instrumented to capture meaningful events, the discovery of strategies and common errors becomes possible using machine learning techniques (Chung and Kerr, 2012). As the number of learning apps and games increase, requiring students to use those apps and games for homework, practice, or other educational purposes may be a compelling way to motivate students to engage with educational content while also providing a source of diagnostic information for teachers. Best practices developed by CRESST researchers on how to integrate math games into the curriculum have included identification of common errors exposed by games, what the errors imply about student understanding, and instructional strategies to bolster students' understanding (Vendlinksi and Buschang, 2012).

Adaptive Systems to Support Personalization

One long-term trend educational technology is moving toward is transmedia whereby learners engage in coherent learning experiences across different media platforms. The US Department of Education's Ready to Learn (RTL) program is spurring the development of young children's transmedia apps, which include games integrated with formal learning media and other educational programming. These technologies will be instrumented to capture learners' interactions, and development of measures of learning or proficiency will be based in part on the learner's interaction with the apps (CPB & PBS KIDS, 2011).

A fundamental issue is the technical quality of measures derived from fine-grained data. There has been little empirical research on how to establish the technical quality of such measures and only recently have psychometricians begun to address this issue (see

Behrens, Mislevy, DiCerbo, and Levy, 2011; Mislevy, in press). A practice recognized as undesirable is to collect "everything" (given the ease with which such data can be collected) and then derive measures post hoc after the data are collected. When developing measures of learning, this approach can be fatal as everything, unless precisely specified by researchers, will be defined by non-researchers and may not be the indicators related to learning or stored in a format suitable for analysis. Much more research is needed on how to derive meaningful measures from fine-grained data. The principal advantage of viewing an interaction as a measurement point is that issues of validity and reliability become central to conceptualizing what to measure, how to measure it, and how the interaction relates to learning processes and outcomes.

Precision is gained through an analysis of the interaction with respect to the cognitive demands of the task, which can expose the contextual information surrounding the interaction that will allow interpretation of the interaction. The use of transaction data is an emerging area of research for educational data mining and learning analytics researchers (e.g., Romero and Ventura, 2007; Baker and Yacef, 2009; Siemens and Long, 2011). The development of robust measures will presumably lead to more effective instructional practices and student learning. Whether diagnostic information is culled from gameplay and reported to teachers to help them decide where to allocate instructional resources or used in adaptive technology-based systems to "sense" when to provide immediate feedback or execute different instructional branching strategies, the availability of high-quality measures will be critical for any precise targeting of instruction.

CHALLENGES AND BARRIERS TO THE ADOPTION OF RELATIONAL DATA MANAGEMENT IN EDUCATION

For years, policymakers, researchers, and practitioners have depended on summary descriptions of aggregated data or on rather primitive analyses of the relationships between static categories of these data as the basis for education related decisions. Too often we have had to resort to variably informed estimates as the basis for decision making—and approach to data management with serious limitations. The development of relational program and student data management systems provides schools increased capacity to document and understand the characteristics of respective inputs and outcomes by categories of students, staff, and programs in relation to differing educational contexts and circumstances. Effective data management systems can make this capacity readily available in "user friendly" formats to people at various levels in decision making. Clearly, solving the recalcitrant problem of reducing differences in the academic achievement of diverse learners can be facilitated by the capacity to use relevant data to inform educational decisions. This renders use of relational program and student data management systems an important component of an informed strategy for closing the achievement gap.

Ten years later, advances in technology have made feasible the large-scale capture, processing, and analysis of students' moment-to-moment interactions with technology-based systems. As education enters the era of big data and transmedia-based learning, the capture of multiple levels of data for an individual that spans system-level, individual-level, and transaction-level data will provide new opportunities to understand student learning to a degree of precision rarely possible before and provide new opportunities to leverage such data to deliver on the promise of personalized instruction.

As we have illustrated, the possibilities and implications of relational data management to improve our understanding of learners and learning and to improve the quality of education overall are many and compelling. Still, there have been a number of roadblocks and challenges in the adoption of such systems. Although the United States remains the only country pushing for electronic medical records (EMR), privacy concerns still inhibit the seamless sharing of medical data nationwide. Indeed, the US Department of Education as early as 2009 began advocating for electronic educational records (EER) in the same model as digital medical records, in the interest of conducting the kind of data analysis that will inform and improve educational intervention and improve outcomes for all learners, but questions about who owns student data remains a sticking point.

A further challenge to achieving the full potential of relational data management in education is the availability of data. In order to realize the types of relational analysis we on the commission would like to see, which takes into consideration the real-time conditional and contextual relationships between learners, teachers, and curricula, we would need far more data than is currently captured in assessment. Data about a student's home life or health, for example, are unlikely to be available in consistent forms and quantities for all students, so that they may easily be captured in a relational database. After all, a database is merely a multidimensional manila folder; its value lies largely in the amount and quality of data it holds.

Still, before we begin pushing for more and more data to be collected ad infinitum, it might behoove us to be clear about what exactly we wish to know. I am reminded of an observation my teacher Donald Hebb made in the 1950s, which has always stuck with me, that we spend a lot of time doing more and more elaborate analysis in order to answer questions that shouldn't have been asked in the first place. One of the problems with data mining is that we now see that we could potentially ask and answer any number of questions but this does not mean that every question is worth asking.

So, what exactly should we be asking of relational data in education? As we explored in chapter 5, there are a multitude of different forms and sources of evidence that can and should be engaged with and orchestrated in the making of judgments and decisions in education. Assessment should be providing these forms of evidence. One of the commission's primary messages was that the decontextualization of assessment evidence is proving to be fallacious—these data points gain their meaning in the context of their relationships to each other, which forces the collection of evidence (assessment is a way of collecting evidence) to be sensitive to both context and relationships, thereby making decontextualization obsolete. What we should be striving for—and what relational data analysis systems and strategies can enable us to achieve—is comprehensiveness with respect to categories of data and contextualization with respect to the manner in which these data are both collected and interpreted.

BIBLIOGRAPHY

Advanced Distributed Learning (ADL). (2009). *Sharable Content Object Reference Model (SCORM)*, Version 2004 (4th ed.). Alexandria, VA: ADL.

Antonenko, P. D., Toy, S., & Niederhauser, D. S. (2012). Using cluster analysis for data mining in educational technology research. *Educational Technology Research and Development, 60*, 383–398.

Bach, C. (2010). *Learning analytics: Targeting instruction, curricula and support services.* Proceedings of the 8th Annual Conference on Education and Information Systems, Technologies and Applications, Orlando, FL.

Baker, E. L. (1997). Model-based performance assessment. *Theory into Practice, 36*, 247–254.

Baker, E. L. (2000). *Understanding educational quality: Where validity meets technology.* William Angoff Memorial Lecture Series. Princeton, NJ: Educational Testing Service.

Baker, E. L., Chung, G. K. W. K., & Delacruz, G. C. (2008). Design and validation of technology-based performance assessments. In J. M. Spector, M. D. Merrill, J. J. G. van Merriënboer, & M. P. Driscoll (Eds.), *Handbook of research on educational communications and technology* (3rd ed.) (pp. 595–604). Mahwah, NJ: Erlbaum.

Baker, E. L., Chung, G. K. W. K., & Delacruz, G. C. (2012). The best and future uses of assessment in games. In M. Mayrath, J. Clarke-Midura, & D. H. Robinson (Eds.). *Technology-based assessments for 21st century skills: Theoretical and practical implications from modern research* (pp. 299–248). Charlotte, NC: Information Age Publishing.

Baker, R. S. J. d. (2007). Modeling and understanding students' off-task behavior in intelligent tutoring systems. Proceedings of ACM CHI 2007, Computer-Human Interaction, 1059–1068.

Baker, R. S. J. d., Corbett, A. T., Roll, I., & Koedinger, K. R. (2008). Developing a generalizable detector of when students game the system. *User Modeling and User-Adapted Interaction, 18*, 287–314.

Baker, R. S. J. d., & Yacef, K. (2009). The state of educational data mining in 2009: A review and future visions. *Journal of Educational Data Mining, 1* (1), 3–17.

Behrens, J. T., Mislevy, R. J., DiCerbo, K. E., & Levy, R. (2011). An evidence centered design for learning and assessment in the digital world. In M. C. Mayrath, J. Clarke-Midura, & D. Robinson (Eds.), *Technology-based assessments for 21st century skills: Theoretical and practical implications from modern research* (pp. 13–54). Charlotte, NC: Information Age.

Bienkowski, M., Feng, M., & Means, B. (2012). *Enhancing teaching and learning through educational data mining and learning analytics: An issue brief.* Menlo Park, CA: SRI International.

Bienkowski, M., Feng, M., & Toyama, Y. (2011). *Summary of findings from data mining industry interviews.* Menlo Park, CA: SRI International.

Campbell, J. P. (2007). *Utilizing student data within the course management system to determine undergraduate student academic success: An exploratory study.* Unpublished doctoral dissertation, Purdue University.

Campbell, J. P., & Oblinger, D. (2007). *Academic analytics.* Washington, DC: EDUCAUSE Center for Applied Research.

Chung, Gregory K. W. K. (2014). Toward the Relational Management of Educational Measurement Data. *Teachers College Record* Volume *116* (11), 1–16.

Chung, G. K. W. K., & Baker, E. L. (2003). An exploratory study to examine the feasibility of measuring problem-solving processes using a click-through interface. *Journal of Technology, Learning, and Assessment, 2* (2). Available from https://ejournals.bc.edu/ojs/index.php/jtla/article/viewFile/1662/1504

Chung, G. K. W. K., de Vries, L. F., Cheak, A. M., Stevens, R. H., & Bewley, W. L. (2002). Cognitive process validation of an online problem solving assessment. *Computers in Human Behavior, 18,* 669–684.

Chung, G. K. W. K., & Kerr, D. S. (2012). *A primer on data logging to support extraction of meaningful information from educational games: An example from Save Patch* (CRESST Report 814). Los Angeles, CA: University of California, National Center for Research on Evaluation, Standards, and Student Testing (CRESST).

Codd, E. F. (1970). A relational model of data for large shared data banks. *Communications of the ACM, 16* (6), 378–387.

Corno, L., & Snow, R. E. (1986). Adapting teaching to individual differences among learners. In M. C. Wittrock (Ed.), *Handbook of research on teaching* (3rd ed.) (pp. 605–629). New York: Macmillan.

Corporation for Public Broadcasting (CPB) & PBS KIDS. (2011). *Findings from Ready to Learn: 2005–2010.* Washington, DC: CPB & PBS KIDS.

Flanagan, J. C. (1969). Program for learning in accordance with needs. *Psychology in the Schools, 6* (2), 133–136.

Fletcher, J. D., Tobias, S., & Wisher, R. A. (2006). Learning anytime, anywhere: Advanced distributed learning and the changing face of education. *Educational Researcher, 36* (2), 96–102.

Glaser, R. (1967). Objectives and evaluation—an individualized system. *Science Education News,* June, pp. 1–3. http://files.eric.ed.gov/fulltext/ED015844.pdf

Glaser, R. (1977). *Adaptive education: Individual diversity and learning.* New York: Holt, Rinehart and Winston.

Gordon, Edmund W., & Bridglall, B. L. (2003). *Toward a relational data management system for education* (Pedagogical Inquiry and Praxis™,

No. 4). New York: Institute for Urban and Minority Education, Teachers College, Columbia University & The College Board.

Heritage, M., Lee, J., Chen, E., & De La Torre, D. (2005). *Upgrading America's use of information to improve student performance* (CRESST Report 661). Los Angeles, CA: University of California, CRESST.

Heritage, M., & Yeagley, R. (2005). Data use and school improvement: Challenges and prospects. *Yearbook of the National Society for the Study of Education, 104,* 320–339.

Herman, J. L., Yamashiro, K., Lefkowitz, S., & Trusela, L. A. (2008). *Exploring data use and school performance in an urban public school district* (CRESST Report 742). Los Angeles, CA: University of California, CRESST.

IEEE Learning Technology Standards Committee (LTSC) P1484. (2006). IEEE P1484.12.3., draft 8, *Extensible markup language (XML) schema definition language binding for learning object metadata.* Retrieved June 1, 2006, from http://ieeexplore.ieee.org/servlet/opac?punumber=10263

Iten, L., Arnold, K., & Pistilli, M. (2008, March). *Mining real-time data to improve student success in a gateway course.* Paper presented at the Eleventh Annual TLT Conference. West Lafayette, IN: Purdue University.

James, D. W., Jurich, S., & Estes, S. (2001). *Raising minority academic achievement: A compendium of education programs and practices.* Washington, DC: American Youth Policy Forum.

Johnson, L., Adams, S., & Cummins, M. (2012). *The NMC Horizon Report: 2012 Higher education edition.* Austin, TX: The New Media Consortium.

Jonassen, D. H. (2010). *Learning to solve problems: A handbook for designing problem-solving learning environments.* New York: Routledge.

Katz, I. R., & James, C. M. (1998). *Toward assessment of design skill in engineering* (GRE® Research Report 97–16). Princeton, NJ: Educational Testing Service.

Kerr, D., & Chung, G. K. W. K. (2011). The mediation effect of in-game performance between prior knowledge and posttest score. In J. Matuga (Eds.), *Proceedings of the IASTED International Conference on Technology for Education* (TE 2011) (pp. 122–128). Anaheim, CA: ACTA Press. doi: 10.2316/P.2011.754–046

Kerr, D., Chung, G. K. W. K., & Iseli, M. R. (2011). *The feasibility of using cluster analysis to examine log data from educational video games* (CRESST Report 790). Los Angeles, CA: University of California, CRESST.

Laesecke, A. (2002). Through measurement to knowledge: The inaugural lecture of Heike Kamerlingh Onnes. *Journal of Research of the National Institute of Standards and Technology, 107,* 261–277.

Lezotte, L. W., & Jacoby, B. C. (1992). *Sustainable school reform: The district context for school improvement.* Okemos, MI: Effective Schools Products.

Macfadyen, L. P., & Dawson, S. (2010). Mining LMS data to develop an "early warning system" for educators: A proof of concept. *Computers & Education*, 54, 588–599.

Manyika, J., Chui, J., Brown, B., Bughin, J., Dobbs, R., Roxburgh, C., & Byers A. H. (2011). *Big data: The next frontier for innovation, competition, and productivity*. Washington, DC: McKinsey Global Institute.

Mislevy, R. J. (2013). Evidence-centered design for simulation-based assessment. *Military Medicine*, 178 (10S), 107–114.

National Academy of Engineering (NAE). (2008). *Grand challenges for engineering*. Washington, DC: NAE.

National Research Council. (2001a). Adding it up: Helping children learn mathematics. J. Kilpatrick, J. Swafford, & B. Findell (Eds.). Mathematics Learning Study Committee, Center for Education, Division of Behavioral and Social Sciences and Education. Washington, DC: National Academy Press.

National Research Council. (2001). *Knowing what students know: The science and design of educational assessment*. Pellegrino, J., Chudowsky, N., & Glaser, R. (Eds.). Committee on the Foundations of Assessment, Board on Testing and Assessment, Center for Education. Division of Behavioral and Social Sciences and Education. Washington, DC: National Academy Press.

Newell, A., & Simon, H. A. (1972). *Human problem solving*. Prentice Hall, Englewood Cliffs, NJ.

Park, O.-C., & Lee, J. (2003). Adaptive instructional systems. In D. H. Jonassen & M. P. Driscoll (Eds.), *Handbook of research on educational communications and technology* (2nd ed.) (pp. 651–684). Mahwah, NJ: Erlbaum.

Plass, J. L., Frye, J., Kinzer, C., Homer, B., & Perlin, K. (2011). *Learning mechanics and assessment mechanics for games for learning* (G4LI White Paper 01–2011). New York: NYU/Games for Learning Institute.

Romero, C., & Ventura, S. (2007). Educational data mining: A survey from 1995 to 2005. *Expert Systems with Applications*, 35, 135–146.

Romero, C., Ventura, S., Pechenizkiy, M., & Baker, R. S. J. d. (Eds.). (2011). *Handbook of educational data mining*. Boca Raton, FL: CRC Press.

Shute, V. J., Ventura, M., Bauer, M. I., & Zapata-Rivera, D. (2009). Melding the power of serious games and embedded assessment to monitor and foster learning: Flow and grow. In U. Ritterfeld, M. J. Cody, & P. Vorderer (Eds.), *Serious games: Mechanisms and effects* (pp. 295–321). Philadelphia, PA: Routledge.

Shute, V., & Zapata-Rivera, D. (2012). Adaptive educational systems. In P. J. Durlach & A. M. Lesgold (Eds.), *Adaptive technologies for training and education* (pp. 7–27). New York: Cambridge University Press.

Siemens, G., & Long, P. (2011). Penetrating the fog: Analytics in learning and education. *Educause Review*, 46 (5), pp. 30–40.

Slowinski, J. (2002). *Data-driven equity: Eliminating the achievement gap and improving learning for all students.* Unpublished manuscript, Vinalhaven Schools, Vinalhaven, ME.

Stevens, R. H., & Casillas, A. (2006). Artificial neural networks. In D. M. Williamson, I. I. Behar, & R. J. Mislevy (Eds.), *Automated scoring of complex tasks in computer-based testing* (pp. 259–312). Mahwah, NJ: Erlbaum.

Tanes, Z., Arnold, K. E., King, A. S., & Remnet, M. A. (2011). Using Signals for appropriate feedback: Perceptions and practices. *Computers & Education, 57,* 2414–2422.

Tyler, R. W. (1949). *Basic principles of curriculum and instruction.* Chicago: University of Chicago press.

US Department of Education (DOE). (2010). *Transforming American education: Learning powered by technology.* Washington, DC: DOE.

van Barneveld, A., Arnold, K. E., & Campbell, J. P. (2012). *Analytics in higher education: Establishing a common language.* Washington, DC: EDUCAUSE Center for Applied Research.

Vendlinksi, T. P., & Buschang, R. E. (2012, March). *Effectively incorporating video games into math instruction: Results from recent field studies.* Roundtable at the Society for Information Technology and Teacher Education, Austin, TX.

Vendlinski, T. P., Chung, G. K. W. K., Binning, K. R., & Buschang, R. E. (2011). *Teaching rational number addition using video games: The effects of instructional variation* (CRESST Report 808). Los Angeles, CA: University of California, CRESST.

Vendlinski, T., & Stevens, R. (2002). Assessing student problem-solving skills with complex computer-based tasks. *Journal of Technology, Learning, and Assessment, 1* (3). Available from http://www.jtla.org.

Wainess, R., Koenig, A., & Kerr, D. (2010). *Aligning instruction and assessment with game and simulation design.* Proceedings of the 2010 Interservice/Industry Training, Simulation, and Education Conference, Orlando, FL.

A STAR TO GUIDE BY: TOWARD ASSESSMENT THAT IS CAPABLE OF INFORMING AND IMPROVING TEACHING AND LEARNING

In this book, we set out to convey the ideas generated by the Gordon Commission on the Future of Assessment in Education, which was itself an effort to connect the leading minds from a number of disciplines so that they might generate a vision for the future of assessment in education. The commission enabled these scholars to do something that had never been done before—launch a two-year-long conversation between psychologists and social theorists, education theorists and philosophers, psychometricians and statisticians, and data scientists and digital innovators to apply themselves toward the problem of what assessment can and should be in the twenty-first century. What they came up with was truly transformative—a vision of not only what assessment should be but also what it can be. In a series of papers, pamphlets, and commentary pieces, in meetings and conferences, they clearly show us that assessment can be the silver bullet in educating to the fullest possible extent all learners in the United States, regardless of their background, socioeconomic status, or place of residence. In other words, this vision of assessment is quite possibly the key not only to equity in academic excellence but also to ensuring the resilience and competitiveness of the United States in a global marketplace.

As we have discussed, many great thinkers in various fields have warned us that the twenty-first century will bring unprecedented transformations to our society. We are already feeling the effects of what the marketplace expects educated workers to be able to do and are beginning to see how technology can enhance or modify human abilities. Despite a steady program of educational reform and despite concerted effort by passionate and committed educators to understand and improve pedagogy in the United States throughout the twentieth century, we have failed to educate all learners in our country. The growing and evermore costly assessment regime we have designed has not only failed to tell us why we have failed in our strenuous efforts but also does not give us the information and tools we need to improve education for all learners in the United States. The Gordon Commission's technical report offers us a truly powerful document (Gordon et al., 2013)—a blueprint for reenvisioning, redesigning, and redeploying assessment so that it does just that.

Here is the crucial point: the Gordon Commission and this book offer a vision for the future, a vision that is rooted in real discoveries and contemporary scholarship, and which is achievable. It does not, however, offer a blueprint for operationalization. With this book, we are inviting you, the people who really bring about change in America, to join our conversation. We are already gaining traction. Although the commission concluded its active work two years ago, we have seen its ideas finding purchase in some of the most influential and prominent circles in education scholarship. *Education Researcher* has published several abstracts of Gordon Commission papers, the *Journal of Negro Education* has reprinted all six papers dedicated to the questions of diversity, excellence, and equity in education, and in November 2014, *Teachers College Record* published a special issue dedicated to its work. It appears that *Harvard Educational Review* will publish a symposium dedicated to discussing the commission's findings and recommendations and the National Academy of Education is in preliminary discussions to convene a standing committee on the future of assessment for education. The many stakeholders in contemporary education—policy makers, administrators, educators, education entrepreneurs and innovators, parents, and students—all stand to benefit from joining this conversation and applying the full weight of American passion, ingenuity, and resources to transforming this vision into a reality.

The Gordon Commission on the Future of Assessment in Education was created to consider the nature and content of American education during the twenty-first century and how assessment can be used most effectively to advance that vision by serving the educational and informational needs of students, teachers, and society. Its report came at a critical and propitious time in the history of US education. The Common Core State Standards in Mathematics and English Language Arts adopted by 45 states and the District of Columbia, as well as Next Generation Science Standards, are currently being rolled out in schools all over the country. The Common Core State Standards stress problem solving, creativity, and critical thinking over the memorization of isolated facts and decontextualized skills. Assessments meant to embody and reinforce those standards are under development and will be given for the first time in this year. Over the next few years, states will be deeply engaged in implementing the standards and preparing for the new assessments. These developments have heightened awareness among educators and state and federal policy makers of the critical relationships among more rigorous standards, curriculum, instruction, and appropriate assessment, and have created an opportunity to address issues of long standing.

THE GORDON COMMISSION'S FINDINGS

The commission developed a four-dimensional approach to understanding assessment—its nature, its purposes and uses, how it is constructed, and how it is practiced. These are summarized below.

Nature of Assessment

1. Assessment is a process of knowledge production directed at the generation of inferences concerning developed competencies, the processes by which such competencies are developed, and the potential for their development.
2. Assessment is best structured as a coordinated system focused on the collection of relevant evidence that can be used to support various inferences about human competencies. Based on

human judgment and interpretation, the evidence and inferences can be used to inform and improve the processes and outcomes of teaching and learning.

Purposes and Uses of Assessment

1. The Gordon Commission recognizes the difference between (a) assessment *of* educational outcomes, as is reflected in the use of assessment for accountability and evaluation, and (b) assessment *for* teaching and learning, as is reflected in its use for diagnosis and intervention. In both manifestations the evidence obtained should be valid and fair for those assessed and the results should contribute to the betterment of educational systems and practices.

2. Assessment can serve multiple purposes for education. Some purposes require precise measurement of the status of specific characteristics while other purposes require the analysis and documentation of teaching, learning, and developmental processes. In all cases, assessment instruments and procedures should not be used for purposes other than those for which they have been designed and for which appropriate validation evidence has been obtained.

3. Assessment in education will, of necessity, be used to serve multiple purposes. In these several usages we are challenged to achieve and maintain balance such that a single purpose, such as accountability, does not so dominate practice as to preclude the development and use of assessments for other purposes and/or distort the pursuit of the legitimate goals of education.

Constructs of Assessment

1. The targets of assessment in education are shifting from the privileging of indicators of a respondent's mastery of declarative and procedural knowledge toward the inclusion of indicators of respondent's command of access to and use of his/her mental capacities in the processing of knowledge to interpret information and use it to approach solutions to ordinary and novel problems.

2. The privileged focus on the measurement of the status of specific characteristics and performance capacities, increasingly, must be shared with the documentation of the processes by which performance is engaged, the quality with which it is achieved, and the conditional correlates associated with the production of the performance.

3. Assessment theory, instrumentation, and practice will be required to give parallel attention to the traditional notion concerning intellect as a property of the individual and intellect as a function of social interactions, acknowledging that knowledge is both individual and distributive and that proprietary knowledge can be both personal and collegial.

4. The field of assessment in education will need to develop theories and models of interactions between contexts and/or situations and human performance to complement extant theories and models of isolated and static psychological constructs, even as the field develops more advanced theories of dialectically interacting and dynamic biosocial behavioral constructs.

5. Emerging developments in the sciences and technologies have the capacity to amplify human abilities such that education for and assessment of capacities like recall, selective comparison, relational identification, computation, and so on will become superfluous, freeing up intellectual energy for the development and refinement of other human capacities, some of which may be at present beyond human recognition.

Practices of Assessment

1. The causes and manifestations of intellectual behavior are pluralistic, requiring that the assessment of intellectual behavior also be pluralistic, that is, conducted from multiple perspectives, by multiple means, at distributed times, and focused on several different indicators of the characteristics of the subject(s) of the assessment.

2. Traditional values associated with educational measurement, such as, reliability, validity, and fairness, may require reconceptualization to accommodate changing conditions, conceptions, epistemologies, demands, and purposes.

3. Rapidly emerging capacities in digital information technologies will make possible several expanded opportunities of interest to education and its assessment. Among these are

a. individual and mass personalization of assessment and learning experiences;

b. customization to the requirements of challenged, culturally and linguistically different, and otherwise diverse populations; and

c. the relational analysis and management of educational and personal data to inform and improve teaching and learning.

THE GORDON COMMISSION'S PUBLIC POLICY STATEMENT FOR A FUTURE OF ASSESSMENT *FOR* EDUCATION

At its conclusion, we on the commission prepared a policy statement that capitalizes on the opportunity to bring about a fundamental reconceptualization of the purposes of educational assessments. The statement itself was prepared by James Pellegrino, cochair of the commission, and Lauren Resnick, member of the executive council, with input from Sharon Lynn Kagan, consultant to the chair, and other members of the executive council—Randy Bennett, Eva Baker, Robert Mislevy, Lorrie Shepard, Louis Gomez, and myself—and with the writing and editorial assistance of Richard Colvin. This public policy statement represents the authors' sense of recommendations that are implicit in the work of the commission. It encapsulates the findings and recommendations of the Gordon Commission as gleaned through its series of consultative conversations and publications and is provided below.

The members of the commission recognize that the future of assessment will be influenced by what the R&D and the assessment production communities generate as instruments and procedures for the assessment in education enterprise. However, we are very much aware that equally determinative of the future will be the judgments and preferences of the policy makers who decide what will be required and what practitioners and the public will expect. In recognition of the crucial role played by policy makers, the policy statement of the executive council of the Gordon

Commission concludes with three recommendations directed at those who make policy concerning education and its assessment.

Transforming Assessment to Support Teaching, Learning, and Human Development

Although assessment, broadly construed, is a central element of education and must be aligned with both teaching and learning goals, it is not the only—or even the major—tool for improving student outcomes. Indeed, for education to be effective, schools must be designed with clear and precise teaching and learning goals in mind and supported in ways that make them likely to reach those goals; teachers must be provided with the appropriate instructional materials and professional development; and other resources including time, technology, and teachers' skills must be deployed strategically.

To be helpful in achieving the learning goals laid out in the Common Core State Standards, assessments must fully represent the competencies that the increasingly complex and changing world demands. The best assessments can accelerate the acquisition of these competencies if they guide the actions of teachers and enable students to gauge their progress. To do so, the tasks and activities in the assessments must be models worthy of the attention and energy of teachers and students. The commission calls on policy makers at all levels to actively promote this badly needed transformation in current assessment practice.

The first and most important step in the right direction will require a fundamental shift in thinking about the purposes of assessment. Throughout the long history of educational assessment in the United States, it has been seen by policy makers as a means of enforcing accountability for the performance of teachers and schools. For a relatively low outlay, assessments could expose academic weaknesses and make it possible to pressure schools and teachers to improve. But, as long as that remains their primary purpose, assessments will never fully realize their potential to guide and inform teaching and learning. Accountability is not the problem. The problem is that other purposes of assessment, such as providing instructionally relevant feedback to teachers and students, get lost when the sole goal of states is to use them to obtain an estimate of how much students have learned in the course of a year. It is critical that the nation's leaders recognize that there are multiple purposes of assessment and that a better balance must be struck among them. The country must invest in the development of new types of assessments that work together in synergistic ways to effectively accomplish these different purposes—in essence, systems of assessment. Those systems must include tools that provide teachers with actionable information about their students and their practice in real time. We must also assure that, in serving accountability purposes, assessments external to the classroom will be designed and used to support high-quality education. Finally, the nation must create a demand for improved assessment practices by helping parents and educators understand the need for change.

The transformation of assessment will require a long-term commitment. There will be some who will argue that, with the work of the Partnership for Assessment of Readiness for College and Careers (PARCC) and Smarter Balanced state consortia to create new assessment systems not yet complete, it would be better to wait before pursuing major policy changes. The commission disagrees and believes that because that work is unfinished, now is the time to move toward more fundamental changes. Certainly, the new assessment systems will need to be implemented and analyzed and then—based on data—revised, to be sure that they are, indeed, supportive of the standards. The fundamental reconceptualization of assessment systems that the commission is calling for should guide those inquiries. The states leading the consortia must demand that the assessment systems be robust enough to drive the instructional changes required to meet the standards. In addition, states have to expect that the assessment systems will provide evidence of student learning that is useful to teachers.

Finally, states have to demand that the systems be flexible enough to be adapted to new methods of delivery and scoring as they emerge. As of now, the funding for the consortia will run out in 2014, just as the new assessment systems are starting to be used, and the costs will likely be shifted to the states. The states will have a financial as well as educational incentive to make sure the assessment systems are working as intended.

Consistent with the above, the leadership of the Gordon Commission has developed a set of recommendations directed toward federal and state policy makers, private for-profit and non-profit organizations related to assessment, the scholarly community, and philanthropists. As a context for these recommendations, we briefly summarize major themes that emerged from meetings that the commission held across the country as well as reviews and syntheses of research regarding assessment history, methods, philosophy, digital technology, and policy.

Reconsidering Assessment: Why, What, and How We Assess

The purposes of assessment fall into two general categories. First, assessment of learning generally involves an appraisal of student achievement after a period of instruction. Such assessments can be used to judge attainment for such purposes as accountability, admission to college or other opportunities, and to evaluate programs or approaches. Second, assessment for learning involves a more restricted and focused appraisal of student knowledge during a shorter period. It is designed for purposes such as adjusting and improving instruction. Although both types of assessment share certain features, each must be tailored to their specific purpose; an assessment designed for one purpose, such as accountability, is seldom best suited for other purposes such as instructional adjustment.

Recognizing that accountability will continue to be an important aspect of educational policy, the Gordon Commission believes that accountability must be achieved in a way that supports high-quality teaching and learning. It must be remembered that, at their core, educational assessments are statements about what educators, state policy makers, and, indirectly, parents want their students to learn and—in a larger sense—become.

What we choose to assess is what will end up being the focus of classroom instruction. Teachers and students will take their cues from high-stake tests and will try to score well on them regardless of their type. So, it is critical that the tests best represent the kind of learning students will need to thrive in the world that awaits them beyond graduation. But changing the nature and quality of external accountability tests will not be enough. An equal, if not greater, investment needs to be made in new assessment resources and tools that better integrate assessment with classroom teaching and learning, and better represent current thinking on how students learn and on changes in the world at large.

The globalization of the economy, advancements in technology, the development of the Internet, and the explosion of social media and other communication platforms have changed the nature of what it means to be well educated and competent in the twenty-first century. Digital technologies have empowered individuals in multiple ways, enabling them to express themselves, gather information easily, make informed choices, and organize themselves into networks for a variety of purposes. New assessments—both external and internal to classroom use—must fit squarely into this landscape of the future, both signaling what is important and helping learners know that they are making progress toward productive citizenry.

More specifically, assessments must advance competencies that are matched to the era in which we live. Contemporary students must be able to evaluate the validity and relevance of disparate pieces of information and draw conclusions from them. They need to use what they know to make conjectures and seek evidence to test them, come up with new ideas, and contribute productively to their networks, whether on the job or in their communities. As the world grows increasingly complex and interconnected, people need to be able to recognize patterns, make comparisons, resolve contradictions, and understand causes and effects. They need to learn to be comfortable with ambiguity and recognize that perspective shapes information and the meanings we draw from it. At the most general level, the emphasis in our educational systems needs to be on helping individuals make sense of the world and how to operate effectively within it. Finally, it is also important that assessments do more than document what students are capable of and what they know. To be as useful as possible, assessments should provide clues as to why students think the way they do and how they are learning as well as the reasons for misunderstandings.

Designing and implementing assessments that support this ambitious vision of education represents a major challenge. Historically, educational assessments have been far more narrowly focused. Assessments have been designed primarily to provide summative information about student, teacher, school, and system performance. That information has been used to highlight weaknesses, direct the spending of money, choose students for additional help or advanced classes, and evaluate the effectiveness of programs or teaching methods. Present testing practices enjoy broad support among policy makers because many people accept them as defining educational accomplishment. But this emphasis on measuring student performance at a single point in time and with assessments whose primary purpose is to provide information to constituencies external to the classroom has, to a large extent, neglected the other purposes of assessment.

Moreover, developing a new mindset about the contexts and purposes for assessment, as well as new approaches to accomplish it, is not only difficult but also requires an investment of resources. Presently, the federal government is absorbing the lion's share of the costs for the systems of assessment being developed by the PARCC and Smarter Balanced state consortia. The conditions of that support stipulate that accountability components be the primary focus of their work. As a result, it is highly likely that the tools and resources needed to support teacher uses of assessment in the classroom will be seriously underdeveloped and in need of significant further work. When this round of federal funding ends and the states are left with the challenges and costs associated with implementation and further development of accountability systems, there may be little money remaining to devote to formative assessment and practices.

Moving Forward: The Opportunity

Because assessments are, essentially, a claim about a student's competencies, new approaches to assessment must be treated as a process of gathering evidence to confirm or disprove particular claims. That evidence, which in a system of assessments can come from multiple sources, can be used to improve both how and what students are learning. The evidence might include activities ranging from simple to complex performance tasks pursued within classrooms as well as assessments external to regular classroom activities.

Digital technologies hold great promise for helping to bring about many of the changes in assessment that the commission believes are necessary. Technologies available today and innovations on the immediate horizon can be used to access information, create simulations and scenarios, allow students to engage in learning games and other activities, and enable collaboration among students. Such activities make it possible to observe, document, and assess students' work as they are engaged in natural activities—perhaps reducing the need to separate formal assessment for accountability from assessment that advances and supports learning in the moment. Technologies certainly will make possible the greater use of formative assessment that, in turn, has been shown to significantly impact student achievement. Digital activities may also provide information about noncognitive abilities—such as persistence, creativity, and teamwork—that current testing approaches cannot.

Juxtaposed with the promise is the need for considerable work to be done on issues of scoring and interpretation of evidence before such embedded assessment can be useful for these varied purposes. Many issues, including some alluded to above, have been discussed and debated among educators and assessment experts for many years. As part of those discussions it is now widely recognized that large-scale standardized testing has exerted a greater and greater influence over American schooling. At the same time, it has been shown repeatedly that teachers have the largest impact on education of any in-school factor. And it is what teachers do, what they teach, and how they assess in classrooms that give teachers that influence. Given that fact, it would seem appropriate to identify specific, effective instructional resources such as curricula and classroom assessments and then prepare teachers to use those resources effectively. However, the notion that education must be locally controlled is deeply engrained in our nation's culture and educational politics and that fact has meant that instructional resources must be chosen by those closest to the classrooms, which sometimes means individual teachers. So, states have individually relied on external tests to exemplify and enforce their content standards so as to ensure some degree of consistency of quality and results across classrooms, schools, and districts in their jurisdiction. External tests, then, have too often become the de facto curriculum with a range of intended and unintended outcomes, such as impoverishing the development and use of effective classroom assessments. The Common Core State Standards, and the rethinking of assessment that they are fostering, provide an opportunity to challenge this deeply held belief in local control.

THE GORDON COMMISSION'S RECOMMENDATIONS TO PUBLIC POLICY MAKERS
In the Realm of State Collaboration and Policy

The constitution of every state in the nation requires it to provide free public education to its children. That means that states have the most authority over the assessments used to monitor the quality of the education children are receiving. Although the past several decades have seen some power and authority over schooling and assessment shift to the federal government, this trend is now in the other direction. The states, acting through the National Governors Association and the Council of Chief State School Officers, demonstrated that they recognized the need for better standards and assessments when they led the creation and adoption of the Common Core State Standards. Although the two assessment consortia are federally funded, they are led by the states. The states participating in the consortia have agreed to establish common progress categories. This record of collaboration is something to build upon. Most state education departments are understaffed and poorly funded. That means that taking on the additional responsibility of monitoring how well the assessments are working will be difficult for them to accomplish on their own. They will have an incentive to continue to work together on this important job.

It is recommended that states create a permanent council on educational assessments modeled on the Education Commission of the States to take on this function. Funding for the council should come from the federal government, states, and a small tax on every assessment sold. The council's first responsibility would be to commission an evaluation of the strengths and weaknesses of the Smarter Balanced and PARCC assessment systems and their effect on teaching and learning. The purpose of this evaluation would be to ensure that the new assessments are, indeed, driving instruction that is consistent with the educational vision embodied in the standards. As has been done before with evaluations of important assessment programs such as the National Assessment of Educational Progress (NAEP), such an evaluation might be conducted by an independent panel assembled under the auspices of the National Academy of Sciences or the National Academy of Education.

In addition, the council should do the following:

- The council should conduct research on how assessments are changing, help inform states so that they make good purchasing decisions, and address issues as they arise. It would also oversee the process of setting cross-state performance-level targets.
- It should mount a public education campaign targeting parents, educators, school board members, and the media explaining the importance of good assessment to quality education.
- It should create a study group on the challenges of equitable assessment to explore issues related to diversity, equity, and excellence.
- It should commission research on policies designed to secure the privacy of assessment data while also creating protocols for making large quantities of such data available to qualified researchers.

In the Realm of Federal Policy

Significant pieces of federal educational legislation are awaiting reauthorization, including the Elementary and Secondary Education Act (ESEA) of 2002 and the Higher Education Act (HEA), which expired in 2013. The reauthorization of these major pieces of legislation provides an opportunity to promote new ideas about assessment. The Obama administration has successfully used incentives built into the American Recovery and Reinvestment Act of 2009, the Race to the Top competitions, and the Investing in Innovation fund to bring about a variety of policy changes and innovations. For example, the Race to the Top district competition requires applicants to use "collaborative, data-based strategies and 21st-century tools" to move beyond one size fits all approaches and personalize learning. This has significant implications for assessments and the type of feedback they provide for teachers and learners. The US Department of Education has used its waiver powers to allow states to experiment with measuring students' year-to-year growth rather than their status at a fixed point in time.

This waiver power was also used to free states from some of the onerous accountability aspects of the NCLB act. It is recommended that the president and Congress consider various models to encourage experimentation with different approaches to assessment and accountability. In reauthorizing ESEA, the Obama administration should press for funds to incentivize states and assessment companies to experiment with radically different forms of assessments, including challenging performance tasks that better represent the learning activities that will help students develop the competencies they will need to succeed in the twenty-first century.

In the Realm of National Research and Development

The assessments that we will need in the future do not yet exist. The progress made by the PARCC and Smarter Balanced state consortia in assessment development, while significant, may still be far from what is ultimately needed for either accountability or classroom instructional improvement purposes. This is not a criticism of the consortia per se but a realistic appraisal of the design constraints and timelines imposed upon their work from the outset. While America certainly can profit from the consortia's work, the US Department of Education, the Department of Defense, the National Science Foundation, and the National Institute of Child Health and Human Development, in collaboration with the philanthropic community, should commit to a ten-year research and development effort to strengthen the capacity of the US assessment enterprise to broaden the range of behaviors, characteristics, and manifestations of achievement and related development that are the targets of assessment in education. This effort should be a partnership between not-for-profit organizations (existing or newly created), the for-profit sector, professional teacher organizations, and universities. There are multiple models for this type of public-private research and development effort in biomedicine, defense, and other fields.

As discussed earlier, one goal of this effort should be the creation of assessment tasks that exemplify the type of learning that we want to occur in classrooms. Today, teaching to the test is seen as a negative consequence of accountability testing. With the proper assessment tools, it will be easier to encourage teaching to the underlying competencies as standard practice. In order to be practical, new ways of delivering and scoring such assessments will have to be developed. Technologies for presenting rich and varied materials and for capturing and automating the scoring of written responses and other student behaviors currently exist and show promise. But they will need to continue to improve and be adapted for a variety of subjects in order for these new assessments to be widely used for a range of assessment purposes.

This expanded view of assessment will require the training and employment of broadly educated specialists in learning, cognition, measurement, and assessment. It is recommended that the government and private philanthropies increase the number of pre- and postdoctoral scholars dedicated to the development of this expertise.

GENERAL RECOMMENDATIONS CONCERNING THE FUTURE OF ASSESSMENT IN EDUCATION

1. As is traditional in the medical profession and is rapidly being embraced as a guide for all professional activity, the recommendation is made that in assessment policy, practice and use of assessment data, this field should "First Do No Harm." Responsibility for honoring this value falls at multiple levels—policy makers,

administrators, staff, and perhaps most heavily on the manufac-
turers of assessment devices and those of us who sell them.

2. We could declare as consensus among the members of the
   commission that assessment can serve multiple purposes. There
   is less agreement concerning the possibility that a single test
   should be so used, however, the consensus holds concerning
   the need for balance in the attention given to the use of assessment for different purposes. It is recommended that with the
   possible exception of "informing and improving teaching and
   learning," no single purpose should be permitted to distort the
   valued goals of education. Similarly it is recommended that
   fidelity to the purpose for which the instrument or procedure is
   designed be honored. This recommendation references, among
   other concerns, the difference between our traditional concern
   with assessment of education and the commission's emphasis
   on assessment for education.

3. Assessment in education is essentially grounded in inferential reasoning. It is a process by which evidences collected for
   the purpose of the disconfirmation of inferences one seeks to
   make concerning the phenomena being assessed. It is therefore
   recommended that assessment processes be held to standards
   similar to those long honored in the tradition of the empirical sciences. However, given the commission's concern for
   changing paradigms and shifting epistemologies, it is further
   recommended that the universal utility of positivist scientific
   methodologies as a standard for evolving assessment practices
   be subjected to continuing inquiry.

4. We believe that most members of the commission embrace concern for differential validities, that is, the idea that validity may
   be a relative construct and that it's relativity must be taken into
   account in policy making and practice with respect to assessment in education. It is therefore recommended that the field
   embrace the notion of differential validities and the imperative
   that tests of validity be appropriate to the populations and situations in which the construct is being utilized.

5. It is recommended that research and development efforts be
   intensified around questions related to the implications for

assessment in education that flow from questions related to the cargo of learning transfer. Special attention may need to be given to the complementarities between mastery of declarative and procedural knowledge and the intentional command of instrumental mental processes.

6. It is recommended that the targets of assessment in education be broadened to include a wider range of human abilities, ways of adaptation, amplified abilities, and human capacities, including those that are the products of exposure to digital electronic technologies.

7. Given the considerable evidence in support of agency, disposition, cultural identities, and existential states as influences on the nature and quality of human performance, it is recommended that research and development concerning the relationships between human performance and these variables be given considerably greater priority in inquiries concerning assessment in education.

8. Debate continues concerning the idea that intelligence is a characteristic of individuals, intelligence is a collectively produced construct best associated with social groups, and the idea that intelligence originates and is expressed in both contexts. The increased practice of collaboration in the production of knowledge and its application suggests the importance of our recommendation that research and development effort be directed at differentiating assessments to capture intellective competence as a property of individuals and as a function of collaboration between persons.

9. Considerable concern has been expressed in the commission about the artificiality of "stand-alone" or "drop-in-from-the-sky" tests. Perhaps more problematic than the isolated character of these examinations is concerned with the tendency to treat the data from these tests as independent and sole sources of information concerning the performance and status of students. Some commissioners argued for the greater use of systems of examinations distributed over time embedded in the ongoing teaching and learning of experiences. It is recommended that assessment in education move progressively toward the development and use of diversified assessment systems for the generation and collection of educational assessment data.

10. It is then the final recommendation, implicit in the work of the Gordon Commission, that the academic and philanthropic sectors of the society—cooperatively supported by tax levy funds, consider the creation of a Virtual Institute on the Future of Assessment in Education (VIFAE) to continue the inquiry initiated by the Gordon Commission, to encourage broad and cross-disciplinary collaboration in this work, and to support the attraction to and development of young and new scholars to conceptual, research and development explorations of the relationships between assessment, teaching, and learning.

Not a Blueprint, but a Star to Guide By

In a short essay he prepared to introduce a special issue of *Teachers College Record* (2014) to the work of the Gordon Commission, Louis Gomez, commission member and professor of education and information science, writes that the Gordon Commission and its ideas offer us a chance to pause and rethink our test-based policies and practices. The commission's work encourages us to ask the question, "What should be the 'true north' guiding assessment into the next generation?"

True north, he writes, points the way to an overarching shared goal. Accountability—identifying who is best—has become our de facto true north. The Gordon Commission asks us to consider whether accountability is the proper true north to guide action as we move toward the middle of the twenty-first century. An identifiable true north has great import for understanding decisions and activities resulting from, or responding to, decisions. A north star places our activity in context. With a clear goal in sharp relief, activity makes sense. For example, if the goal is simple accountability, low-cost, and single point in time, assessments are sensible things to build. With clear goals, a true north, when faced with a new problem, like those that will surely be presented by the Next Generation Science Standards, we know what to do. If accountability is our North Star, the blueprint is clear. We would, in one way or another, know who is best. The chapters in this volume encourage us to take a step back from our current thinking, policies, and activities and to ask ourselves whether the assessments we are building today are the right ones for tomorrow. Is accountability the North Star for the next generation of policy and practice?

Gomez continues, in school organizations around the country, accountability systems, and high-stakes assessments guide practice in the schoolhouse and policy in the statehouse. Scores on these assessments tell us, we hope, that students are learning and that some school organizations, and even states, are enabling students to learn while others are not. Is this what progress should mean to us? Where do we go next? Should we change the question? Rather than asking, "How am I doing?" should we ask, "How can we do better?" What should assessments look like if the improvement of learning and teaching, rather than accountability, were the North Star?

The commission papers and the ideas in this book offer readers the chance to imagine assessment anew. At the core of these deliberations and findings of the commission is a call for researchers, practitioners, and policy makers to come to understand how assessment systems might help educators to incrementally help develop people toward that goal. At the very least, new societal demands ought to give rise to conversations about the appropriate goals for assessment systems. If the field is to make progress, a clear sense of the goal—the true north—is necessary. An overarching message of the commission is that we ought to be asking more of our assessments and of students than knowledge of facts.

Assessments, according to ideas generated by the commission, should be up to the challenge of informing practice in ways that fit the contexts where people learn. Assessments should be able to provide timely information at scales that matter to practice. Assessments should be sensitive to the fact that helping students improve is not only an intellective matter but a social and emotional one as well. People are complex systems and we are actors in a complex system.

Gomez (2014) observes that it will take great scientific accomplishment to effectively craft a new generation of assessments. We don't know how to do it. The old blueprints to construct assessments need to be augmented with new knowledge. Hence, we have a need for a newly articulated North Star. The way forward is uncertain. Every now and again, it is important to pause and ask ourselves, "What is our true north?" This continuing conversation prompted by the work of the Gordon Commission offers us that opportunity.

BIBLIOGRAPHY

Gomez, L. (2014). The Gordon Commission: An opportunity to reflect. *Teachers College Record, 116* (11), 1–4.

Gordon, Edmund W., et al. (2013). *To Assess, to Teach, to Learn: A Vision for the future of assessment: Technical report.* Princeton, NJ: Educational Testing Services. http://gordoncommission.org/rsc/pdfs/gordon_commission_technical_report.pdf

INDEX

accountability, 1, 6, 10–11, 16,
    20–2, 23, 25, 30, 37, 40, 102,
    111–12, 133, 152
achievement gap(s), 13, 16, 17, 68
    See also diversity
achievement test. See standardized
    testing
affective processes. See cognitive
    processes
agency (human), 59–60, 67–8,
    75, 80
assessment
    alternate and new approaches
        to, 2, 5, 10, 19, 20–2, 24,
        26–8, 29–31, 32, 36, 37–41,
        45, 47–9, 50, 53, 76, 77–83,
        94, 97–103, 107–8, 109–14,
        107–35
    design of or purposes and targets
        of, 4, 44–5, 47–9, 52–4, 90,
        91–100, 149–54
    traditional approaches to, 6,
        17–18, 21, 26–8, 29, 35, 37,
        40, 97, 100–1, 108–9, 114,
        137
    See also dynamic pedagogy,
        formative assessment, Gordon
        Commission, measurement
        science(s), standardized testing,
        summative assessment
attribution or attributional processes.
    See cognitive processes

behaviorist theory, 15, 97
    See also cognitive processes

chaos theory, 21
cognitive processes
    and assessment, 15, 150
    emerging epistemologies
        regarding, 25, 35, 37, 39–41,
        43–6, 60, 69–70, 74, 93–4, 97,
        99–103
    relevant to learning, 25, 45, 69,
        71, 74–6, 78–80, 97, 119–24,
        128–9
Cognitively Based Assessment of,
    for, and as Learning (CBAL).
    See formative assessment
Coleman report, 9, 14, 20
College Board. See standardized
    testing
Common Core, 4, 10, 15, 22–3,
    24–6, 27, 90
Common Core State Standards.
    See Common Core
comprehensive education, 21, 70
content mastery. See subject-matter
    mastery
context, or conditional correlates
    of human performance, 6, 68,
    103, 122, 150
contextualizing assessments,
    52–3, 63, 77
emerging epistemologies
    regarding, 6, 26, 37, 38–40,
    41–2, 69, 97, 109
technological developments that
    enable assessment to account
    for, 48–9, 98–9, 163, 173
See also decontextualization

cosmopolitanism, 73
curriculum
    development, design and
        conceptualization of, 15, 17,
        61, 63, 72, 78, 96–7, 126–8
    and learning, 79, 82, 108,
        116–19
    See also cognitive processes,
        Common Core, dynamic
        pedagogy, education, higher-
        order thinking, NCLB,
        pedagogical troika, subject-
        matter mastery
curriculum-embedded assessment.
    See assessment, formative
    assessment, proximal assessment

data
    big data *or* digital ocean, 49, 100,
        149, 162
    privacy concerns, 22, 52, 100,
        162–3
    quality of, 95, 98, 103, 149–50,
        162–3
    sources and types of, 69, 98–100,
        150–2
    See also relational data analysis,
        standardized testing: qualitative
        analysis of standardized test
        data, validity
decontextualization, 26, 27, 39, 42,
    48, 49, 97
    See also measurement science(s),
        standardized testing
diverse learner population.
    See diversity
diversity (response of assessment to),
    9, 10, 28, 55, 152–3
    and equity in education, 13, 14,
        46, 115, 134–5, 137–8
"dropped-in-from-the-sky."
    See decontextualization,
        standardized testing
dual process theory, 74
    See also cognitive processes

dynamic pedagogy, 24, 79–83,
    108–9, 114–35

education
    changing paradigms of, 7,
        35–41, 61–2, 67–70, 76–83,
        97, 100–1, 114–19, 147–50,
        152–3
    and democracy, 16–17, 63–4,
        71, 90
    goals of, *or* purposes of, 61–4,
        117, 119–20
    reforms, 12–16, 19–25, 31, 54–5,
        118
    See also Common Core,
        standardized testing
Elementary Secondary Education
    Act, 14
empiricism. *See* positivism
engagement, 69–70, 75–8, 81,
    99–100, 121–2, 126–7, 180
    See also agency (human), cognitive
        processes
evidence-centered design, 45, 47,
    90–1, 94–5
evidentiary argument *or* evidentiary
    data source(s) *or* evidentiary
    reasoning in assessment, 49,
    53–4, 90–1, 93–103
    See also assessment,
        evidence-centered design

Flexner Report, 36
formative assessment, 31, 81–2, 92,
    108–14, 125, 133
    See also assessment

generalizability theory, 44
    See also assessment, standardized
        testing
Gordon Commission on the
    Future of Assessment in
    Education
    background of, 1–2, 4–5,
        24–5

policy recommendations of,
    174–89
vision of, 3–4, 5, 11, 17, 19, 30,
    31, 40, 54–5, 61, 169–74

higher-order thinking, 4, 16, 25,
    27, 61, 73–5, 77, 96, 117,
    123–5
    See also Common Core, dynamic
    pedagogy, intellective
    competence, metacognitive
    functioning, twenty-first
    century: competencies
high-stakes testing, 12, 14, 22, 63,
    98, 109
    See also standardized testing

individualization, 53–4, 68, 115,
    156–7, 160–1
intellective competence, 3, 7, 10,
    11, 25, 27, 30, 45–6, 53, 55,
    77–83, 119–20, 123–8
intelligence, 7, 16, 35, 60, 127
    See also higher-order thinking,
    intellective competence,
    intelligence testing, knowledge,
    metacognitive functioning
intelligence testing, 12, 18, 79,
    89–90, 137
item response theory, 44
    See also assessment, standardized
    testing

knowledge
    and knowledgeability, 72–5
    and understanding or intellective
    competence or mental abilities,
    6–7, 12, 24–5, 27, 30–1, 35,
    37–9, 71–2, 75, 81–2, 102–3,
    120–1, 122, 126
    See also subject-matter mastery,
    twenty-first century

learning analytics. See context,
    individualization

measurement science(s).
    See also intellective competence,
    processual analysis
    historic uses in assessment, 17,
    21, 29, 42, 147–8
    new developments in, 9–11, 26,
    28, 29–33, 44–6, 93–4, 101
meritocracy, 6, 13, 28
metacognitive functioning, 25, 71,
    80, 83, 109, 123–5, 127

National Assessment of Educational
    Progress (NAEP), 13
Next Generation Science Standards.
    See Common Core
No Child Left Behind (NCLB), 15,
    63, 153
    See also curriculum, education,
    standardized testing
nonacademic capacities, 62, 64, 68,
    74–5

orchestration, 103, 117, 163

pedagogical troika (assessment,
    teaching and learning), 29–32,
    40–1, 54–5, 78–9, 101–2, 107,
    112, 114–19, 130
    See also assessment, dynamic
    pedagogy
performance assessments, 15
    See also standardized testing
Planning-Programming-Budgeting
    System (PPBS), 14
positivism or positivist tradition in
    assessment, 41–2, 90, 94, 148
    See also accountability,
    decontextualization,
    measurement sciences
postmodern test theory, 53
    See also assessment: design of
probe(s). See assessment
Problem Solving in
    Technology-Rich Environments
    (TRE), 134

processual analysis (as function of
    assessment), 10–11, 18, 26,
    28, 32, 36, 114–15, 116–19,
    137–8, 148–50
    See also Gordon Commission
    on the Future of Assessment:
    vision of
proximal assessment, 115–16
psychometrics, 44–6, 101, 133
    See also measurement sciences

relational adjudication, 41
    See also intellective competence,
    twenty-first century:
    competencies
relational data analysis, 147–50,
    152–61
    challenges and barriers to
    adoption, 161–3
    examples of relational data
    management systems, 154–6
    See also assessment: new
    approaches to, big data,
    individualization, technologies
    relevant to assessment

Scholastic Aptitude Test (SAT).
    See standardized testing
situative processes. See cognitive
    processes
standardized testing, 7, 10–11, 13,
    14, 19, 22, 17, 37, 53, 92,
    117, 133
    history of, 12–16, 89–90, 137
    qualitative analysis of standardized
    test data, 19, 90, 135–40
    See also assessment: traditional
    approaches to, Common
    Core, education, measurement
    sciences, positivism
standards-based reform (SBR), 15,
    23, 135

See also Common Core,
    curriculum, standardized
    testing
string theory, 21
subject-matter mastery, or
    content mastery, 7, 27, 32,
    69, 74–5, 81–2, 102–3,
    118, 122
summative assessment, 92, 108–9
    See also assessment: traditional
    approaches to

technologies relevant to education
    and assessment, 40–1, 46–9,
    50–3, 65–6, 71, 73, 76,
    77–9, 94, 98–103, 133–4,
    147–63
transfer, 27, 44, 50, 52, 55, 74, 122
    See also higher-order thinking,
    intellective competence,
    knowledge, subject-matter
    mastery
transformative theory, 70
    See also cognitive processes,
    knowledge
twenty-first century
    being educated in, 70–83
    challenges, 3, 38, 42–3, 50, 61,
    63, 65, 71, 75
    competencies or skills, 4, 17, 24,
    38, 40, 53, 59–62, 72–6, 77–8,
    79–82, 96–7, 118–20

validity, 11, 21, 26–7, 19, 39, 51,
    90, 92–3, 94–5, 100, 134
    See also assessment, evidentiary
    argument, positivism,
    standardized testing,
    technologies relevant to
    assessment
veridicality
    challenges to, 7, 21

CPSIA information can be obtained at www.ICGtesting.com
Printed in the USA
BVOW06s1036010916

460834BV00028B/99/P

9 781137 519955